S0-CYD-666

OFF AND RUNNING

Tony seized her by the shoulders and tried to kiss her. Charly struggled to get free and twisted her head so his lips touched her ear.

Heavy footsteps pounded on the graveled path, and strong arms abruptly ended the embrace. They looked up to find Kevin Marlowe glowering at them both.

"You've damn well forgotten your manners and your breeding!" he said to Tony. "But then," he added, scowling at Charly, "I know precisely who to blame for this incident. Don't think I haven't seen the lures you've been casting for my brother."

Charly stared at him, momentarily helpless and shaken. "It—it is not what you think!" she said before she could stop herself. "It was all a plan. I wanted to show Bella what Tony is really like. That he'd flirt with anyone!" She rallied, and defended herself. "I did not encourage him that much!"

Kevin raised his eyebrows. "He is a healthy young man and you showed him a willing female. If you must play with fire, pick someone old enough to know the rules."

And before she realized what he intended, he pulled her into his arms and kissed her himself, thoroughly.

PAPERBACK TRADE INN
230 S. Main
Clawson, MI 48017
(248) 288-4660

ATTENTION: SCHOOLS AND CORPORATIONS

WARNER books are available at quantity discounts with bulk purchase for educational, business, or sales promotional use. For information, please write to: SPECIAL SALES DEPARTMENT, WARNER BOOKS, 666 FIFTH AVENUE, NEW YORK, N.Y. 10103.

**ARE THERE WARNER BOOKS
YOU WANT BUT CANNOT FIND IN YOUR LOCAL STORES?**

You can get any WARNER BOOKS title in print. Simply send title and retail price, plus 50¢ per order and 50¢ per copy to cover mailing and handling costs for each book desired. New York State and California residents add applicable sales tax. Enclose check or money order only, no cash please, to: WARNER BOOKS, P.O. BOX 690, NEW YORK, N.Y. 10019.

Racing Hearts

EILEEN WITTON

WARNER BOOKS

A Warner Communications Company

for Russell

WARNER BOOKS EDITION

Copyright © 1988 by Eileen Witton
All rights reserved.

Warner Books, Inc.
666 Fifth Avenue
New York, N.Y. 10103

Ⓦ A Warner Communications Company

Printed in the United States of America

First Printing: November, 1988

10 9 8 7 6 5 4 3 2 1

CHAPTER

One

*T*he determined rays of the morning sun shone through the lace hangings at the window fronting on Vesey Street, casting an enchanting tracery of light and shadow across the Turkish carpet. Mrs. Charlotte Deane was in no mood to appreciate this display. She perched uneasily on the edge of a brocade sofa in the drawing room of one of the most elegant mansions in New York City. With no little trepidation, she regarded the lined face of the elderly man seated by the desk before her. His next words could spell her salvation—or her utter ruin.

Pieter Van Bleek took a delicate pinch of snuff from his enameled box, then fastidiously dusted away a few stray flecks that fell on the Mechlin lace of his wristbands. An old-fashioned gentleman he was not one to decide hastily. Charlotte could only hope that this time his careful deliberation would weigh in her favor.

He tented his fingertips and frowned at her through square-rimmed glasses that reflected the flickering firelight from his hearth. Everything about him, from his powdered, curled wig and the wide skirts of his wine velvet coat to the large silver buckles on his high-heeled shoes, bespoke his preference for the elegant age just past. His long waistcoat, richly laced with gold thread and with quilting that outlined the pattern of full-blown lilac roses, was a thing of marvelous beauty. Furnishings created by the Scotchman Duncan Phyfe spoke quietly of long-established wealth and comfort.

He can afford this, Charlotte told herself as she tried to stop her nervous fingers from knotting and reknotting the strings of her reticule. She swallowed, gathering her courage. "I . . . I ask only an extension," she informed him with every bit of persuasiveness she could muster. "One more year."

Van Bleek tapped his fingertips together in a manner that made her swallow convulsively. He gave a small, dry cough. "The turn of this century has brought many changes," he intoned, and coughed again, this time in mild disapproval. "I have noted that it has become the custom in New England for a widow to continue the business of her late husband. But a horse breeding farm! I cannot consider that an occupation for a delicately nurtured female."

Charlotte lifted her determined chin. "For this female it is, sir. Give me that year, and I will make a success of the farm."

Van Bleek stretched out his legs and crossed his thin ankles. "My dear child—"

"I am fully six-and-twenty, Mr. Van Bleek. I am no longer a green girl but a capable woman. I can do it. One year; is that so much to ask?"

He cleared his throat. "As I remember, your late husband, Abner Deane, had an unusually good stallion at the time of our agreement." he consulted a sheet of paper. "Summer Storm, I believe the animal was called. Mr. Deane was well on his way—or so I understood him to say—to producing a winning line of racehorses."

Charlotte took a deep breath to steady her voice. "I still have that stallion, sir. And several of my mares carry his offspring and will foal in the coming months. My two-year-old, Summer Wind, is the first of his colts, and will soon prove that his sire's speed is handed down to his progeny. I shall enter him in the race meet at Maidenhead in a few months' time, and he is sure to be a winner." Her conviction rang clearly in her words.

"That is as may be, Mistress Deane. Still, I cannot but

have reservations. What can a woman know of raising and training racehorses?''

She bit back the acid retort that sprang to her lips. Her wretched temper! She must not give way to it now, when everything she loved hung in the balance. How was Mr. Van Bleek to know that Deane Farm had literally been under her management for the last five years? Abner Deane, at least so far as business matters were concerned, had been nothing more than a figurehead. But Mr. Van Bleek could never acknowledge ability and intelligence in a mere female.

''I have Ben Stokes,'' she said, providing him with an answer that he could accept. ''He has been our manager and trainer from the very beginning. I am sure you must be aware of his capabilities. So you see, not that much has changed at Deane Farm.''

Van Bleek picked up the folder of legal papers he had drawn from the safe in the corner and raised penetrating eyes to meet Charlotte's. ''If, as you say, the farm is to be left in Mr. Stokes's hands, as it always has been . . . we shall see.'' He consulted the papers he held, then looked at his visitor once more. ''I have had no report on the condition of Deane Farm since the death of your husband a year ago. I would be foolish, would I not, to grant an extension of a loan on property I have not inspected?''

Charlotte swallowed, trying to calm the agitated nerves that gripped in her stomach. ''If you would care to drive out there . . . ?'' she began.

He waved her suggestion aside. ''I am not, as you must be well aware, expert in raising horses. With your permission, I will arrange for an acquaintance of mine, whose opinion I have good reason to trust, to visit your farm. If he says all is well, you may have your extension.''

''When . . . when may I expect him? I am staying in New York at the moment, at the home of my aunt, Augusta Hanley, but I can drive out to the farm to meet him.''

Mr. Van Bleek consulted the clock on the mantelpiece. ''Shall we say this afternoon? I am sure you, as well as I, would like to see this business settled quickly.'' He rose. ''If all goes well, I shall see you again in the morning.''

With an effort, Charlotte smiled at him. Her property was

in excellent order; she had no need to worry. But still, she could not be easy until the precious extension was actually signed and safe in her possession.

The butler showed her to the front door, and she stepped out into the crisp morning air. Not success, but not failure, either. Her sister Bella eagerly awaited her return to their Aunt Augusta's home, where everyone was involved in the final preparations for a grand ball to be given the next evening. Well, they would have to do without her for a while. She would return there only long enough to have old Bruno harnessed to her light chaise, and be off on the half-hour drive to her farm.

She started down the steps, then paused, her attention caught by a gentleman astride a loose-limbed roan hack. The animal approached with the most bone-jarring, stiff-pasterned trot it had ever been her misfortune to witness, yet the rider was easy in the saddle. With more than a touch of admiration, Charlotte noted the perfect harmony between horse and rider. It went beyond the ability of a natural horseman, she acknowledged with a silent salute. Here, in this man, was that rare blend of athletic ability and purely intuitive understanding of the peculiarities of his mount.

His riding dress was impeccable, from the slightly military cut of his coat of olive green drab down to his buckskin breeches and the extraordinary gloss on his riding boots. His figure set it off to advantage, being, in her eyes, perfectly proportioned as to height and breadth. Every inch of his bearing proclaimed him a buck of the first stare, a gentleman—and a horseman of note.

The man scanned the houses, peered over at the number posted just to Charlotte's right, and reined in with no visible movement. The horse stopped sweetly. The gentleman looked about, signaled to a street urchin, and entrusted his mount into the lad's care. Crossing the street, he paused at the base of the stairs, waiting for Charlotte to complete her descent.

Recollecting herself, she hurried down. Two steps from the street she stopped, for she found herself staring directly into his scowling features. No trace of the patience and love of horses he must possess showed in his expression. This was not a man she would care to cross! She caught herself pitying whoever—or whatever—had caused his ill-temper. But people who visited Mr. Pieter Van Bleek were often in grave difficulties.

A sudden half-smile, as intriguing in its unexpectedness as in its singular charm, transformed the man's cynical expression. Charlotte caught her breath. Charming, indeed! For the first time, she was glad for the black veil that hid the soft color flushing her cheeks.

He tipped his hat to her, accompanying the gesture with a slight bow. The movement sent a thick lock of dark hair tumbling over his forehead, and he brushed it casually back with a well-formed hand. Becoming hints of gray just touched each temple, and that slight smile lingered in the depths of his brown eyes.

Charlotte descended the last two steps, allowing him to pass. Without sparing her another glance, he replaced his hat and proceeded up to the house.

Respectable widows draped in black crepe were rarely accorded more than common politeness by gentlemen. It was with the oddest sensation of regret that she hailed a passing hackney and took her seat. Giving the direction of her aunt's home on Beaver Street, she sank back against the squabs.

What a horseman that man must be! She closed her eyes, allowing her imagination free rein. How she would love to see him taking a powerful horse over hurdles. He wouldn't thrust the animal or ride *ventre a terre*, throwing his mount off stride. Nor would he need to bully or coax. The horse would move with him naturally, for they would be one body, one mind, an inseparable team, taking the course together: the Compleat Horseman . . .

Charlotte gave herself a mental shake. She had no time for such fanciful daydreams. She had done what she could with her visit to Mr. Van Bleek. Tomorrow night her little sister Isabella would be presented to the New York beau monde at the ball given by their aunt. For the time being, she must forget her problems and turn her thoughts to finding Bella a suitable husband.

Meanwhile, Charlotte's Compleat Horseman was ushered into the drawing room she had just left. Pieter Van Bleek rose at once, coming around his desk to take his visitor's hand.

"So you are Kevin Marlowe," he declared, beaming. "A pleasure, sir! It seems odd, does it not, that we have not met face-to-face before now? I feel we have been acquainted these last five years."

"And so we have, sir." Kevin Marlowe shook his host's hand. "We've certainly been joined in enough business ventures to feel ourselves old friends."

"Do sit down, my boy." Van Bleek gestured to the sofa, then resumed his own chair. "What may I do for you? I must say, it was quite a surprise—a very welcome one, I might add—when I received the letter yesterday announcing your visit."

"I had not expected to be obliged to travel as far as New York," Marlowe admitted. He leaned against the cushions, resting one elegantly booted leg over the other. "I am looking for my brother, and I hope you may be able to help me."

"Your brother?" Mr. Van Bleek raised his eyebrows.

"Yes. He left England suddenly, and so far I have traced him to Boston. There I learned he had been seen much in the company of one George Bingham and that the two had departed their lodgings the day after my arrival. Young Bingham's parents are residents of New York City, or so I've been told, and I hoped you could provide me with their address so I may take the rascal back home."

"I see." Van Bleek tented his fingertips once more. Charlotte would have recognized this sign of his hesitancy. "I collect you are not making a stay in our fair city?"

Marlowe gave a short, mirthless laugh. "I leave as soon as I have collected that jackanapes brother of mine and settled his debts."

Van Bleek sighed. "Ah, then you would not have time to do me a favor," he said, almost to himself.

"What is it?" Marlowe asked at once. He might be anxious to be off, but the other man was not one to ask favors lightly.

"It would not take long." Van Bleek eyed him hopefully. "You are an expert in raising horses, are you not?"

Marlowe grinned suddenly. "You wish to purchase a mount?"

"I need someone I can trust to make an assessment for me." Briefly, he outlined the history of Deane Farm.

"A widow, carrying on such a business?" Marlowe frowned in disapproval. "Best just foreclose and be done. It will be a failure."

Van Bleek shook his head. "She is a very determined young woman. You might have seen her, for she left just as you arrived."

Marlowe considered. "I did. And I remember thinking it was a damnable business that widows were left in need of the services of money lenders. But it seems this one brings it on herself."

"Oh, it was her husband who arranged the original loan. She merely asks an extension of a year. I would like to give it to her, but first I need someone to make sure the farm has not gone to ruin in the time since her husband's death."

"And that someone is myself?"

Van Bleek spread his hands, rings sparkling in the firelight. "If you do not wish to do it, I am sure I can find someone else, but if you do have the time to spare, there is no one whose judgment I trust more in such matters. As her purpose is to breed racing animals, I believe you would be an excellent judge of her stock."

Marlowe nodded, intrigued in spite of himself. It would be interesting to see an American breeding and racing stable. "When would you like me to go?"

"This afternoon, if it would not be an imposition."

The gentlemen lingered a little time, talking of mutual concerns; then, armed with the directions to both his brother's friend and Deane Farm, Kevin Marlowe took his leave. If he rode straight to the widow's stable, using that bone-jarrer he had made the mistake of hiring, he could locate that good-for-naught brother of his by early afternoon. With luck, they could leave New York City in the morning and be on their way back to England within days. The thought went a long way to cheering him.

As Marlowe rode along Broad Way, the late morning haze

gave way to a beautiful, sunny noon. He soon left the flat rock paving behind and entered a rolling countryside of farms and trees. There were more unpleasant ways of spending a day, he decided. He passed a brewery, the last of the landmarks Van Bleek had listed, and slowed his mount to a ragged trot. After they had rounded a bend, he urged it to the top of another low hill.

Below him, clustered at one end of sprawling green fields, lay a collection of stone and timber buildings. He drew his mount to a halt, his gaze running in approval over the excellent layout. No wonder Mrs. Deane wanted to keep this farm. It was a beautiful sight. A square house, set over a high stone basement with an attractive piazza running the full length of the front, stood back from the lane, shielded by a row of elm trees. Three barns, bordered by rail fence paddocks, lay behind. Beyond stretched acres of pastureland, with a stream winding its peaceful way along a fence line. Scattered horses grazed contentedly.

As Marlowe rode into the yard, a woman, who must have been waiting, stepped from the house. The soft dove-gray folds of her merino walking gown fell gracefully about the ankles of her half boots, and she wore a simple straw bonnet. Such a delicate little creature to take on such a job! It didn't seem right to him. But that, he reminded himself, was none of his concern. Pieter Van Bleek merely wanted confirmation that his investment was in good repair.

Her eyes widened in surprised recognition as he neared. Beautiful eyes, he decided, a clear, crystalline blue, wide apart, and set beneath delicate brows. An intriguing face, in all, for there was more than mere prettiness here. There was a great deal of character, as well. If she weren't a recent widow, and if he weren't here on business, he might pass an agreeable half hour or so.

He swung down from his saddle and came forward. "Mrs. Deane? Pieter Van Bleek asked me to pay you a visit."

"You are to inspect the farm, sir?"

He smiled. "From what I can see, everything appears to be in good order. I am sure this is the merest formality.

Kevin Marlowe at your service, ma'am,'' he added, by way of introduction.

"Charlotte Deane." With an odd hesitancy she offered him her hand, then called a groom to see to his horse. "Now," she said, "where would you like to begin?"

"The stable, Mrs. Deane." He started toward the back of the house and she fell into step beside him. Everywhere, he noted with approval, neatness prevailed. Puddles of rainwater still lay on the ground, but the walks were designed with stepping-stones so that sure footing could still be found. The buildings, too, showed signs of being kept in excellent repair.

"It is all very new," he commented.

"It was completed less than five years ago," Charlotte told him. "My husband began building shortly before we were married, and we made a few changes as we went along, to make it more practical."

They reached the first pasture, where a number of yearlings grazed in the new grass. Marlowe leaned against the top rail, watching, a slight smile of contentment on his face.

All seemed to meet with his approval, Charlotte noted with relief. She felt her tension ease, only to be replaced by an unnerving awareness of his presence. He was an overpowering man, she decided, with a strength of mind she could almost feel. And yet there was a gentleness about him as he watched the yearlings run, a feeling for the animals that was nearly overwhelming. No wonder his mount responded to him so willingly, as if falling under his spell. Even she was being . . .

What she was being was nonsensical. He would approve her extension, inform Mr. Van Bleek of his findings, and that would be the end of that. All that mattered was that he liked Deane Farm. And there was no reason why he should not! The only alterations that had taken place since the death of Abner Deane were for the better. She looked about, trying to see the farm as it would appear to a stranger, without the sense of peace and home that it always held for her. It was beautiful, she decided, though she knew she was prejudiced.

"Well, I suppose we should have a look at your breeding

stock,'' Kevin Marlowe said at last, with a touch of regret. ''Where is this stallion of yours?''

''In the far pasture, by the lane.'' Lifting her skirts slightly as they walked through the wet grass, she led the way, trying to ignore that disturbing awareness of the man moving beside her. His manner was brisk and businesslike, and she must not forget the reason that he was here.

They reached the next fence, but the stallion was not there. Frowning, she looked about, finally spotting a stolid lad pushing a barrow. ''Henry!'' she called. ''Where is Summer Storm?''

''Mr. Stokes is still exercising him, Mrs. Deane,'' the youth replied. ''I did go to look for him as you asked, but never found him.''

Charlotte sighed. ''I am sorry, Mr. Marlowe. We had little warning of your visit.'' And if Mr. Van Bleek had not doubted the abilities of a mere woman, Mr. Kevin Marlowe would not be there at all! Suddenly, her earlier irritation returned. She could grudgingly understand why Mr. Van Bleek wanted the property inspected, but she could not help feeling insulted. Why did she have to justify herself to a stranger! As if her neighbors—or even her rivals on the track—could not vouch for the excellence of her property and her horses!

''I have no idea how far my manager has taken the stallion, or when they will be back,'' she told him.

''It can't be helped, then. Have you only the one stud? Is there not another?''

''I have not yet found one to equal Summer Storm. As Mr. Van Bleek may have told you, I am trying to breed a line of superior racehorses. To use a less than perfect stallion would be sheer folly!''

''That it would,'' he agreed. ''And how has your program fared so far?''

''We are only just now seeing the results, but the first colt, Summer Wind, has all the speed and stamina for which I bred.''

Marlowe nodded. ''Van Bleek told me you depend on an upcoming race meet to prove the worth of your line. All hangs on one colt? What if the horse doesn't win?''

"He must!" Charlotte declared hotly, then realized how desperate she must sound. "He will," she corrected herself. "There is not a horse in all of New York to equal him."

Marlowe returned no answer, and she eyed him nervously. They had reached the next pasture, where her mares, many heavy in foal, were turned out. Her favorite, a gray named Zephyr, seeing Charlotte approach, whickered softly and trotted up to the fence.

Charlotte reached out, stroking the velvet nose that nudged affectionately at her. "Hello, old girl. Everything all right?" The mare blew grass-stained breath down the front of her dress, and Charlotte sidestepped with the expertise of long experience.

"How many horses do you have?" Marlowe asked suddenly.

"Besides my stallion and Summer Wind, I have seven yearlings, and these dozen mares," she told him. "And nine foals are due over the next few months, the first any day now."

"For what you have in mind, you need more stock," he declared bluntly. "Not every foal will inherit the best points of sire and dam."

There had been more, but she was not about to tell him of the mares she had been forced to sell to pay the bills—and the mortgage payments. Instead, she managed a smile. "It is the same as with a stud. An inferior mare will not add to the excellence of my line. I am constantly looking out for promising horses. When I find one good enough, I will buy it."

The gray horse moved to the water trough that stood nearby. Charlotte ducked under the fence rails and Kevin Marlowe followed her.

"This is my best mare," she admitted, watching fondly as the horse drank. "I have great hopes for her foal, if it is a colt, as an eventual replacement for his sire."

"I am told your husband pledged the land for the loan. Why?" he demanded abruptly. "It seems a very foolish arrangement. If you cannot meet the mortgage, you stand to lose everything."

"He needed the money to build the house and barns,"

she said steadily, defending Abner rather than answering his question.

The mare, having had her fill, began to play in the trough, throwing her head and splashing the water high. "Zephyr, no!" Before Charlotte could stop her, the horse tossed her head once more, sending a sheet of water flying over their visitor.

He jumped back, but too late. Water dripped down his face, and both his coat and waistcoat were liberally splattered. He shook his arms, shedding droplets.

"Oh, Mr. Marlowe!" Charlotte exclaimed in dismay. It was a shocking thing to have happen to one's guest—particularly one who held such power over her! If he should be displeased, or angered . . .

"Your mare does not seem to approve of my coat," he remarked, with what seemed to Charlotte amazing mildness under the circumstances.

"I am so sorry! Please, come up to the house. We will see what my housekeeper can do for you."

"Thank you, but no." His smile was somewhat tight. "I prefer to leave my clothing in the hands of my man. I find I have complete trust in his abilities." He wiped at his face with an almost dry sleeve. "The damage is not that bad."

Still, Charlotte could not be happy until she had convinced him to accept a towel at least. He declined her invitation to come into the house, and instead waited near the kitchen door until she returned. He gave himself only the most cursory mopping, then handed the damp cloth back to her.

"I believe I will not take up any more of your time, Mrs. Deane. There is a pressing matter I must take care of in New York this afternoon."

"You will see Mr. Van Bleek?" She realized she held her breath.

He looked down on her through half-lidded eyes. "I am afraid I must."

A sudden chill crept over her. "You cannot mean you will refuse to approve the extension because my mare has spoiled your coat!"

"You may rest easy on that score. The mare was hardly at

fault, but my dear Mrs. Deane, I could hardly approve an extension. It seems to me that your entire future rests on whether or not your Summer Wind proves the worth of his sire. If he does, your yearlings will bring real money. If he does not, it seems to me that you are fairly well ruined. You have not enough stock, nothing to fall back on. You must see that the entire affair is far too risky. It would be sheer folly in me to approve it."

CHAPTER

Two

*C*harlotte stared after Marlowe's departing figure, stunned. To lose her farm—her horses—her very life!—by the casual words of one heedless, unthinking man! He had taken but a perfunctory look at Deane Farm. Did he not realize that his thoughtless decision would destroy her? How could he be so oblivious to what this extension meant to her, so indifferent to her need?

In shock, she walked into her house and stood gazing blindly at the delectable cold nuncheon laid out by her housekeeper. She could not eat. She might never eat again! The mantel clock in her parlor struck two, waking her from her daze. Two o'clock. If she left at once, she could be back in New York well before three. Mr. Van Bleek would still be in his office. She could make one more plea! Running back outside, she shouted for Jim, her hired boy, to put Bruno to the chaise once more. In less than fifteen minutes, she was on the road into town.

It would be her words against those of that odious man, and she would not go down without a fight! She urged old Bruno into a trot.

By the time she reached Vesey Street, Marlowe had come and gone. Van Bleek greeted her with a trace of surprise.

"Mrs. Deane! I was on the point of writing to you." He held out a chair for her. "Mr. Marlowe has given me a report on your property. He considers that although your buildings and land are in excellent condition, you do not have enough stock to make a success of your business."

Charlotte forced her feet into the floor and gripped the arms of her chair in an effort to conceal her emotion. "Mr. Van Bleek, please let me—"

He fixed her with those piercing eyes and coughed gently, interrupting. "I have decided, however, to grant you a few more months, in which time you should be able to dispose of your assets and settle your affairs." He held out a sheet of paper neatly covered by his elegant copperplate script.

Charlotte took the paper in a trembling hand and read it quickly. Six months! Not the year she wanted, but enough. It would carry her past the Maidenhead meet and give Summer Storm's colt the chance to prove his speed. She had a reprieve in spite of that insufferable man!

Tucking the precious extension into her reticule, she thanked Van Bleek profusely and took her leave, her head in the clouds. This would show the odious Mr. Marlowe! She gave herself up to happy daydreams as Bruno plodded down Broad Way toward Aunt Augusta's stately brick mansion on Beaver Street. She would be in time for tea, and she couldn't wait to tell her aunt the good news.

She was admitted at once by Jensen, the elderly butler who had served her aunt for as long as Charlotte could remember. He permitted himself a smile of welcome as he took her pelisse.

"Mr. Treadwell is with Miss Hanley, madam."

Charlotte sighed ruefully. Jonathan Treadwell had been an unwanted suitor at the time of her come-out, before her marriage to Abner Deane. Fighting down a craven impulse to go straight up the stairs instead, she went into the drawing room.

Miss Augusta Hanley's chair had been fitted with wheels so that she could be moved easily. The frail, white-haired lady sat perfectly erect, her chin, every bit as determined as Charlotte's, thrust out, and her patrician nose. raised. A wool rug lay across her knees, undoubtedly placed there by the mousy Miss Nidbury, her faithful companion, who sat in the farthest corner of the room with her interminable needlework.

Miss Nidbury was engaged, as Charlotte well knew, in embroidering a fire-screen of her own design, a depiction of George Washington in the guise of Saint George annihilating a dragon that bore a suspicious resemblance to both the lion and the unicorn of England. Miss Nidbury, though outwardly silent and retiring, held decidedly strong views. Beneath her calm exterior seethed a hotbed of patriotism. Charlotte threw her a smile and approached Miss Hanley.

"Charly, dearest, there you are!" Her aunt hailed her, waving a gnarled, clawlike hand that glittered with rings. "I have just been telling dear Jonathan of your mission. How did you fare?"

Treadwell, cutting a pompous figure in his best brown velvet coat and breeches, rose to his feet. He bowed stiffly, thereby endangering a precariously balanced teacup and saucer. Firmly, Charlotte stifled a comparison of his fastidious fussiness with the easy elegance of that incredible—but odious!—horseman. No matter what irritating qualities Jonathan Treadwell might possess, he would never refuse a helping hand—if he should perceive it to be within his gift.

"Your servant, ma'am. I trust all is now well?" His expression indicated that he trusted no such thing.

Charlotte's smile tightened but remained firmly in place. Sorry to disappoint you, she thought. "Yes, indeed," she said aloud. "Do be seated again, Jonathan, before you upset tea all over Aunt Augusta's Wilton carpet."

This so flustered him that she was compelled to spring forward and relieve him of the cup before he spilled it down the front of his Sunday waistcoat. Charlotte placed it safely on a small table and sat down herself, accepting a cake proffered by her aunt.

Glancing up, she caught Treadwell's gaze resting on her with patent approval. Her dove-gray merino walking gown trimmed with black ribands perfectly suited her role as a widow about to emerge from deep mourning.

If only he had arrived a half hour later! Charly thought mischievously. Then, instead of the morbidly correct garments she had donned for her interview with Mr. Van

Bleek, she would have been dressed in a pink muslin tea-gown with rose velvet ribands. That would have shocked Jonathan's sense of propriety!

"So it seems Mr. Van Bleek has indulged you," he intoned sententiously. "I would not have believed it possible. That farm has been a thoroughly mismanaged affair from beginning to end. You must know that I most strongly advised Abner not to put up the land itself as collateral for the loan to build the house and barn on the same property. You now stand in grave danger of losing all!"

"A feather-witted man," agreed Augusta Hanley briskly, "but one now gone, thank God." She glanced upward piously.

Jonathan Treadwell frowned at this unseemly derogation of one no longer living. He let it pass without remark, however. Miss Augusta Hanley might, in his opinion, be an original, but her position in New York society was unassailable.

Charly, watching the play of emotions on his all too expressive countenance, interpreted them correctly and was hard pressed not to giggle.

"Charlotte!" Her aunt suddenly turned gleaming eyes on her as the import of Treadwell's words sank home. "Do you mean you have been granted your extension?"

"I have, dearest." Charly sank onto the small settee beside the wheeled chair, thus allowing Treadwell, who had been forced to remain standing with his empty saucer clasped in his hand, to be seated also. Charly thoughtfully handed him back his teacup. "Mr. Van Bleek has said he will not foreclose at once. I have six months to make good. And I shall."

Treadwell's brows snapped down, but being too polite to initiate an argument in the presence of Miss Hanley, he changed the subject. Then, as the proscribed time for his visit ended, he rose once more and took formal leave of his hostess. Charly politely accompanied him out into the hall, where he stopped before the front door and turned to face her fully.

"Charlotte."

She sighed, resigned. "Yes, Jonathan?"

"My dear Charlotte, you must know there is no need for

you to struggle so to support yourself and your sister. You have only to marry me to be free of all your troubles.''

She shook her head firmly. "Thank you, Jonathan, but no. I have no wish to marry again. This extension will give me time to prove myself—or rather, for Summer Storm to do so—for that is what it amounts to. When Summer Wind wins, it will prove the worth of his sire."

Charly reached for the door knob, but he stayed her hand. "Is that all you have to rely on? The ability of one stallion?"

"It is enough." She drew a deep breath. "It would all be impossible without Summer Storm. Never could I find another horse of his quality in all of America!"

Treadwell sniffed. "It depresses me that you count on that animal. The beast is vicious! It should have been shot at once when it killed your husband."

"That was not Summer Storm's fault!" Even as she flew to the defense of her beloved stallion, she knew Treadwell was partially right. But the blame lay with Abner as well. Always overly confident, he had not hesitated to put a horse broken only for flat racing to jump a high fence. When Summer Storm refused, Abner Deane was thrown.

"Any horse would have bolted," she declared. "If Abner had not worn spurs, his foot wouldn't have caught in the stirrup and he would never have been dragged. Summer Storm was terrified when he couldn't free himself."

"Be that as it may." Treadwell looked his stuffiest. "You must know you cannot continue with this racehorse breeding nonsense. The idea is absurd! Stop it, I beg of you, and marry me."

Charlotte sighed again. "Jonathan, you must not think that I do not appreciate your kind offer. I am deeply honored, but as I have told you time on end, I do not intend to remarry. I will go on, for Abner's sake. This breeding program was dear to his heart."

"But you did not love the man!" Treadwell shook his head, exasperated. "Why must you persist in his folly?"

Charlotte looked at him quietly. "Because I did *not* love him, Jon. Surely you can see that."

"You are being foolish beyond permission to let a sense of guilt ruin your life!"

"It was my dream as well as his, the one thing we shared. And I will succeed for him, for both of us. One day, American horses will equal any in Europe. And in the meantime, Zephyr will foal within a week or so. If she produces a colt, I may have a stallion to equal even his great sire."

Treadwell, thoroughly vexed, puffed up and blew out his reddened cheeks. "It is no work for a female! You must give it up! It is not at all the thing for a lady of your quality. You are stooping to vulgarity!"

Charly's lips tightened. Without a word, she opened the door and stepped back, waiting. Spluttering both arguments and apologies, Treadwell went out, hesitating on the porch. She shut the door firmly in his face.

She stalked down the hall, only to be brought up short at the drawing room door. Augusta Hanley beckoned imperiously to her.

"Charlotte, my dear," she called anxiously. "I pray you do not intend to whistle that one down the wind."

Charly went at once to her side and bent to kiss a withered cheek. "Oh, but I most certainly do, dearest Aunt. Can you honestly see me tied for life to that shattering bore?"

Augusta cast her a worried glance. "He would make you a good husband, Charlotte. He is a wealthy man, and kind into the bargain. Abner Deane was neither and left you naught but a sea of troubles. You deserve the security. Do not judge all men by Abner's standard."

Sinking down onto the settee beside her aunt, Charly reached over and patted the crippled hand that rested on the arm of the wheeled chair. "I know you mean well, love, and undoubtedly it would be in my best interests to marry Jonathan. But really, I cannot. My father arranged one loveless marriage for me and I have sworn never to enter into another."

She squeezed the hand gently. Aunt Augusta was truly concerned, she knew, and had the welfare of both Charlotte and her sister Isabella at heart—but it was *her* version of their best interests, not Charly's.

Augusta Hanley, her father's youngest sibling, was only too anxious to do all that she could for her two nieces, and she had opened her house to Charlotte and Isabella for the New York Season. Although confined to a wheeled chair by a pernicious arthritic condition, the lady had insisted on managing the seventeen-year-old Isabella's come-out, as she had done for Charlotte nearly eight years before.

"I refuse to take no for an answer," she had informed a protesting Charly. "Bella is far too pretty to waste, isolated as the two of you are on that farm. It is only a half-hour carriage drive from here, so you may come and go as you please, though it must be your duty to chaperon your sister at any party not held in this house. I know I cannot keep you long from that dratted farm of yours, but you owe it to Bella to allow her to reside with me during the Season."

With thankful tears in her eyes, Charly had bent to kiss her forehead. "You must know, my dearest aunt, that you have just granted Bella's every wish!"

Now, forcing her memories from her mind, Charly rose briskly. "I will manage, dear Aunt. I have Ben Stokes, Henry, and Jim to do all the work, and I will cope with the business problems. And now I must see to the final arrangements for Bella's ball. Tomorrow night will come before we know it."

As she turned toward the hall, she glanced out the front window. The sight that met her gaze brought an amused sparkle to her bright blue eyes. "Oh, I am truly off," she said with a ripple of laughter in her voice. "I see General Parks walking up your steps. Behave yourself, now! You must not be forever flirting with your gentlemen friends. It is not in the least seemly in one of your tender years."

With a final light kiss on her aunt's cheek, she hurried to the housekeeper's room. She couldn't help but think as she went of the difference between General Parks, who, she was sure, called to entertain Aunt Augusta so that she herself could concentrate fully on the preparations for the ball, and Jonathan who could never imagine anyone thinking that his call might be inconvenient.

Charly was soon immersed in the many tasks at hand. She so hoped that Bella's entrance into society would be a success, for her sister dreamed of true love and happy endings. Yet, a happy ending for Bella would mean an empty life for Charly. The farm would be lonely without Bella's cheery chatter.

The following morning dawned on a scene of utter chaos in the three-story, slate-roofed brick house on Beaver Street. Jensen, his usually neat gray hair in ruffled disorder, trotted to and fro, intercepting tradesmen with cases of champagne and arguing about the orders while overseeing the placement of an awning over the front walkway and the laying of a strip of red carpeting on the steps. The housekeeper bustled between the dining room below and the ballroom at the head of the stairs, where a footman and the kitchen boy sat on the floor washing the lusters from the huge chandelier that hung in the center of the long room. A dais at the far end was being prepared for a string ensemble from Rochester.

Isabella bounded from one room to another, her eyes twin sapphire stars, as she bubbled with anticipation.

"Bella!" Charly protested as the girl spun gaily about the ballroom, in which potted plants were being arranged. "Go and lie down, or you will be too exhausted to enjoy yourself tonight."

"What, and miss a single moment?" Bella seized her sister about the waist and whirled her around. "Oh, no! This is all for me! My very own come-out! Oh, Charly, I never thought it would ever be!"

Tears momentarily dimmed the sparkle in Bella's eyes, and Charly took her firmly in hand. "Silly goose, you will be worn to a shadow by dinnertime and too tired to dance a step. Now, up you go to rest, or you will look a veritable hag tonight!"

That did it. Bella went, and somehow, after her departure, a sort of desperate orderliness descended on the final preparations.

Thirty sat down to dinner that evening in Augusta Hanley's grandiloquent dining room, and Charly looked about the

table in quiet content. The guests included the cream of
New York society, carefully selected by Aunt Augusta from
those who would have daughters of their own to present—
and therefore would invite Bella to their balls—and those
with the most eligible sons.

The ball itself began at ten o'clock. Bella, almost rigid in
her ecstasy, stood just inside the door of the ballroom,
between her aunt's wheeled chair and Charly, and was
introduced to the seemingly endless line of well-wishers as
they came in. Her eyes, wide and glittering, took in the
elaborate finery and resplendent dress of their guests.

But to Charlotte, filled with pride for Bella's delicate
loveliness, no one could appear more beautiful than her little
sister. Her long curls, paler than the honey color of Charly's,
were piled on top of her dainty head and falling in ringlets
over one bare shoulder. Charly herself had brushed and
pomaded them until they shone like liquid gold. Excitement
brought a delicate pink flush to Bella's cheeks and a glow to
eyes that reflected the celestial blue of her satin gown, high
waisted and open in front to reveal a rosebud-embroidered
sarcenet underdress. Tiny puffed sleeves barely touched her
shoulders with wisps of gauze laced with gold thread. In her
trembling hands she held a nosegay of pink and white roses
presented to her, with an old-fashioned sweeping bow, by
General Parks.

Nor was she the only one in high looks. Tonight, after
more than a year in deep mourning, Charly had dressed in
colors for her role as chaperon. She might have spared
barely a thought for her own appearance, but the pearly
orange-blossom crepe gown, edged in pomona green ruch-
ing that matched her satin slippers, set off her own fair
daintiness to perfection. But as far as Charly was concerned, this hour belonged to Isabella.

The string quartet struck up the music for the first
cotillion. The sisters left their post by the entrance, and in
moments Isabella was claimed by General Parks to formally
open the festivities. Charly slipped away to take up her
duties as hostess.

Glittering light from a hundred candles in the cut-crystal
chandelier bathed the dancers in a warm, flickering glow.

Lilting music filled the long ballroom, and laughing voices echoed from the throng whirling about the floor. Charly circled the room, procuring partners for the next set for every bashful maiden left by the wayside. Satisfied at last that all were enjoying themselves immensely, she stepped back among the chaperons to view the scene. Aunt Augusta must be in ault, she thought with a smile. Her ball was truly a hostess's dream. At least her aunt and Bella were happy... and Mr. Van Bleek had seen fit to ignore the suggestions of that odious Mr. Marlowe. Even now, disappointed as she was in her Compleat Horseman, she felt a little thrill at the memory of his perfect seat on that raw cob. A man who could ride like that...

A delightful laugh rang out, clear and merry, above the strains of music from the dais at the far end of the room. Bella. A slight frown creased Charly's brow. Several dancers were between them and she could not look over their heads, but she knew without seeing that her lively sister flirted daringly with her partner. Out of Charly's sight—and censure—Bella was quite capable of being carried beyond the line of propriety in her excited state. If she was not careful, she risked earning herself the reputation of being fast. Charly began to work her way toward Bella's side of the hall.

Another dance had just begun. There was little hope of catching Bella's attention until it finished, so instead Charly went to the refreshment table. After signaling Jensen to bring more champagne, she filled two glasses and returned to Aunt Augusta's side.

That lady still sat in her wheeled chair by the stairs, where she could greet late arrivals. The position also provided an excellent view of the proceedings. In dressing her mistress, Miss Nidbury had done full justice to the occasion. Aunt Augusta's watered satin robe in shades of lilac and mauve overflowed the chair in rippling folds. The tremendous paniers had been laid aside, there being no room for this excess of fashion between the arms of her chair. A froth of white lace fichu covered her shoulders and was fastened at the bosom of her lavishly embroidered stomacher by knots of ribbon and a cluster of impossible purple silk roses.

Niddy had topped her crown of white hair with a glorious turban of purple gauze adorned with lavender ostrich plumes and a huge amethyst brooch.

Charly presented her aunt with the champagne. "My, but you are grand tonight! The focus of all eyes! Never have I seen you so magnificent."

"Yes, you have. I wore this gown at your own come-out." Augusta Hanley's sharp eyes rested thoughtfully on her niece. "It's good to see you in colors once more, even though I had to give a ball to achieve it."

Charly smiled. "And such a ball. A regular crush! So many people . . . and so many notables . . . I have to congratulate you, dearest."

"We had as many at your come-out . . . and at your wedding ball," Augusta added, watching Charly closely. "It is time we were thinking of that again, and I do not mean only for Bella. You know the proverb, one wedding begets another."

Charly shook her head firmly. "No, thank you, love. I have enough to occupy my life. I have my farm and my horses." She swallowed convulsively. *So far . . .* "That is all I need," she finished.

Aunt Augusta pursed her lips. "For now, perhaps. But what of later? When Bella marries, you will be alone. Accepting Jonathan Treadwell would provide you with companionship, children . . . and a way out of all your financial difficulties, as well. Truly, Charlotte, he is an excellent catch."

"Then *you* marry him." Charly dropped a kiss on her wrinkled cheek and moved off, suddenly unable to preserve a cheerful front. She recognized again that sensation of emptiness, which she quickly stifled. When Bella married, the farm would be very lonely, but the girl must find someone wealthy and influential who would assure her all the elegancies of life! Constant worrying over meeting tradesmen's demands aged one rapidly, Charly reflected ruefully. But Bella must marry for love, not wealth alone. Charly knew too well the sorrows of an arranged marriage such as her father had forced on her. And with Abner Deane, even the promise of financial security had vanished.

The dance ended, and Charly moved to intercept Bella, only to find her sister was no longer in sight. The little minx! she thought. Where could she have gone? She turned toward the dais as the music struck up once more. A rapid search showed that Bella was not in any of the sets that were forming. And neither, she noted with resignation, was a very shy young damsel of her acquaintance, who was seated by herself on a rout chair next to the wall. Remembering her duties as hostess, Charly looked about for an unattached young gentleman whom she might introduce to the timid Miss Decker.

She turned quickly toward the refreshment table and bumped into Jonathan Treadwell, resplendent in black satin knee breeches, white waistcoat, striped stockings, and with both neckcloth and collar so high he could barely turn his head.

"Charlotte," he began, "I have been searching for you. Will you do me the honor of standing up with me in this set?"

She frowned in impatience. "No, really, Jonathan. Can you not see I am both hostess and chaperon this evening? I do not dance."

"Oh, you are angry with me still." He tried to take her hand but she quickly pulled it away. "I fear the depth of my ardor has led me to be premature." His head bent humbly. "Forgive me. I should have waited to declare myself until now, when I see you have at last put aside your mourning garb. You are right to have refused to countenance my improvident proposals until the proper time had passed. Your delicacy of feeling does you great honor." He bowed and attempted a laugh. "You must think me a most callow boor."

For a moment Charly was sorely tempted to tell him exactly what she did think of him, but she decided she had not the time. The timid Miss Decker still sat alone, unclaimed, and her duty called. A happy solution presented itself.

"Ah, Jonathan, you are exactly what I need!"

Before that gratified—and astonished—gentleman realized why he was needed, she presented him to the young lady and he, bound by the dictates of courtesy, had to solicit Miss Decker's hand for the forming country dance.

And that is that, Charly thought, washing her hands of both. Now for Bella . . . but even as she turned, her sister came into view.

Bella, her face flushed and her eyes aglow, tripped lightly up to her. "Oh, Charly," she exclaimed as soon as she came into earshot. "I have met the most wonderful man! He is everything I ever dreamed of! Never have I laid eyes on one so handsome! Charly, I have found the one man for me!"

Oh no, Charly thought. She had been afraid of this, afraid that her impressionable little sister would fall in love with the first good-looking man to pay her court. Bella longed for a Prince Charming who would one day come riding up and carry her away on his great white charger. But Charly had hoped that, with so many eligible gentlemen in New York City, Bella would not fix on one quite so soon.

"Oh, my love! Do not say so! The Season has just begun." She managed a light laugh, hoping to distract her sister with the promise of more delights to come. "You will meet many men before the Season is over, perhaps even more handsome than this one."

Bella laughed with her, a happy, wondering sound. "No, never. Not like Tony."

Charly stiffened. "Tony? You use his given name already?"

"Oh," Bella flushed. "Anthony M . . . Martin. He . . . he asked me to call him Tony."

Charly's tone was chill. "And I suppose you are to be Bella?"

"No. Oh, no." Abashed, Isabella demurred. "He is not so forward as that! I am Miss Hanley to him. But you see, he is hiding from his older brother, who is now in Boston, and he must use another surname. He says he forgets to answer to it, so everyone must call him Tony."

"Indeed," Charly managed to answer, knowing a deep foreboding. To her, this sounded too smokey by half. She could not like the idea of a young man who behaved in so havey-cavey a manner.

"You must not think there is anything wrong!" Bella

urged, as she sensed her sister's displeasure. "It is just that he must make his fortune before his brother finds him."

Or marry one, Charly suspected. Well, he would not succeed here! He must have his eye on their stud farm, not realizing it was mortgaged to the hilt and depending for its rescue on a single stallion. She felt unaccountably relieved. When this fortune hunter learned that fact, he would drop Bella quickly enough.

"And only think, Charly, his brother breeds horses in Ireland." Bella prattled on, sure that this would make the young man acceptable in her sister's eyes. "He has a great stallion named Excalibur who wins all the steeplechases, so Tony knows all about racing horses! You must meet him at once. Let me bring him to you."

Bella skipped off, leaving Charly preparing to be at her most austere and forbidding. She could not allow Bella's heart to be broken by an unscrupulous fortune hunter! She would break up this affair before it ever got started.

Then she saw the young man Bella led by the hand, and her heart sank. This, she realized, was not going to be easy.

CHAPTER

Three

M r. Anthony Martin was beautiful; no other word was adequate. His eyes were bold and dark, and his carefully touseled black hair curled over a wide forehead above chiseled features that would do credit to a Greek god. He bent over Bella, listening to her eager remarks and smiled, slowly, devastatingly, with a flash of perfect white teeth. He epitomized every young maiden's dream of a romantic hero. Charly gazed at him in deepening dismay. There was no doubt in her mind but that he was an expert in the art of dalliance.

He walked toward her, a slim figure in faultless evening dress. Not a dandy perhaps, but obviously a smart. His coat appeared molded to an excellent frame, tall, broad shouldered and slim hipped. Too tall, she decided. And he displayed a lamentable fondness for too much buckram wadding in the padded shoulders of his coat. His narrow waist, also, did not meet with her approval, for it was nipped in more than she could like. But these flights of fashion were no more extreme than those adopted by half the aspiring young Tulips in the room.

On the whole, she much preferred the clean-cut, solid appearance of her Compleat Horseman. But what on earth made her think of him? There was a similarity of coloring between the two men—and both must be in desperate need of money for one sought an heiress, the other a money lender.

For all that, the young gentleman with Bella displayed no want of assurance. Not for a moment did Charly doubt his supreme consciousness of his own appeal, his power over the opposite sex. He could not be more than twenty, she realized, but already he appeared completely confident of his acceptance in any society. Moving across the ballroom floor with the grace of an athlete, he drew the eyes of every female he passed.

He stopped before Charly and made a magnificent leg with the practiced aplomb of a London beau. His smile, as he rose from his bow, blended to a nicety his admiration and a proper touch of deference. Charly nearly gasped, utterly unprepared for his overwhelming charm.

Dear God, she thought in dismay, keeping Bella out of his clutches was going to be nearly impossible!

Bella, her voice trembling with pride, seemed to speak from far away. "Charlotte, may I present Mr. . . . Mr. Anthony M . . . Martin to you? Mr. Martin, my sister, Mrs. Deane."

She barely heard Bella's stammered introduction. Young Mr. Martin took the hand she extended in a warm, firm grip, then his lips brushed her fingertips.

"Your most obedient servant, ma'am," he murmured, his soft voice deep, with a slight musical lilt. Somehow, he made the stock phrase sound sincere.

As if she didn't have troubles enough, now this dashing young buck had to come and compound them! His character was shady . . . he was a fortune hunter, very possibly a libertine! And why, on why, did he have to be so . . . so damnably attractive? She had to do something—but what?

Words failed her, but as she stood there, staring up at him in dismay, she was saved by the musicians. The opening chords of the next dance sounded and a set began to form near them. Mr. Anthony Martin excused himself with another devastating smile and led a radiant Bella onto the ballroom floor. Without conscious thought, Charly again fled to the protection of her Aunt Augusta's side.

Miss Augusta Hanley patted the chilled hand that Charly laid on the arm of her chair. "What a beautiful young man that is, dancing with Bella. Do they not look delightful together?''

''Do you know him?'' Charly demanded.

With smug complacency, Miss Hanley regarded the young couple who were just now coming down the center in the pattern of the country dance. ''Rather a pretty pair, are they not?'' she remarked, oblivious of the urgent note of Charly's question. ''He shows her off well.'' She gave a satisfied grunt. ''Our Bella bids fair to be the belle of her first ball!''

''Never mind that. How does that young man come to be here? Surely you could not have invited him!''

''The Binghams brought him. Do you not remember? No, you were no longer at my side.'' She patted Charly's hand again, but her fond eyes remained on her other niece, who now performed, with her partner, the half-turns of the ''hands across'' at the top of the set. ''I believe he is a friend of their son's.''

''But do you know anything about him? About his family?''

''I believe Mrs. Bingham said that he came over from Ireland quite recently. His brother owns some sort of estate there.''

''An Irishman! But he spoke as an English gentleman. I heard no brogue.'' Or had she? That slight melodious timbre in his voice that could set an impressionable maiden's heart fluttering . . . and Bella was far too impressionable!

Augusta Hanley nodded. ''Oh, he is English. Mrs. Bingham says he is of the first respectability, though I fear he cannot be well off, for he is now staying at the General George Inn.'' She wrinkled her aristocratic nose in distaste. ''I understand him to have been visiting the Binghams but left yesterday to take up lodgings of his own in town. Mrs. Bingham asked if he might be of her party and as an extra man is always an asset at a ball, I assured her he would be most welcome.''

''Yes.'' Even to herself, Charly's answer sounded somewhat flat.

There could be no doubt of his welcome by the young ladies at the ball, she thought wryly. His behavior was all for which a hostess could wish. Though he stood up the allowable two times with Bella, it seemed that he would scatter his favors for the rest of the evening, dancing but once with each of the other girls to whom he was presented.

Charly, keeping a close and not too friendly eye on him, was forced to acknowledge that he behaved just as he ought. And Bella . . . She turned, looking for her sister. There she was in the next set, laughing delightedly up into the face of a middle-aged gentleman of somewhat homely aspect. At least she did not languish when Mr. Anthony Martin was not at her side.

"My nevvy."

Charly turned to find General Parks standing beside her. "I beg your pardon?" she asked blankly.

"Fellow dancing with your Bella. Richard Cranford. Came up for a visit from Philadelphia rather unexpectedly, so I brought him along."

"Of course he's welcome, but I am sure Aunt Augusta has already told you both that." Charly smiled at him, wondering what he was up to.

"Lawyer, you know," the general told her. "Quite a respectable practice in Philadelphia. Well-to-do."

"You must be proud of him," she responded promptly as a sudden suspicion took possession of her mind. Aunt Augusta was matchmaking. "Is he not married?"

General Parks beamed. "Confirmed bachelor, or so he claims. Just never met the right female, that's all. Now, a pretty, lively chit like our Isabella there could make any man sit up and take interest. Our families have long been friends. Do you not think it is time there was a more formal connection between us?"

Had the families been friends? Certainly the general himself had been around for as long as Charlotte could remember, and his visits had become more frequent after the death of her father. But his wife had died many years ago, and Charly was barely acquainted with any of his other relatives. She stole a glance up at his face and caught an odd look of melancholy in his expression.

"Why has there not been a connection before this?" she asked, suddenly following a strong scent.

General Parks shook his head. "You never knew your grandfather, my girl. Proud old bird. Your father was much

like him. Would never countenance a match between a
Hanley and a common soldier.''

"I am quite familiar with their ideas on appropriate
marriages,'' she informed him somewhat tartly. Then her
voice softened. "From something Aunt Augusta once told
me, I gathered that she refused the match her father arranged.''

General Parks nodded slowly. "That she did.''

"And she never married anyone else. I have often wondered why not, when she must have been courted assiduously.''

"She was and all,'' the general agreed, a reminiscent
light kindling in his eyes.

"It is rather sad to see her spend her last years alone,''
Charly continued. "She could yet marry.''

General Parks shook a finger at her. "Your grandfather
would turn over in his grave to hear you suggest such a
thing.''

"Well, if he did, no one would know it, would they?''
Throwing him a mischievous, challenging smile, she turned
back to watch her sister and the general's nephew. There
was, after all, no reason why there should not be two
connections between the families.

She considered Bella's partner with care. Mr. Richard
Cranford must be thirty if he was a day, and by no stretch of
the imagination could he be called handsome. What chance
did such a man have against an Adonis like Anthony
Martin? Still, he must have some charm, for Bella certainly
enjoyed her dance with him. As she watched, he bent down
to murmur something in the girl's ear, which set her off into
a merry peal of laughter.

"Bit of a ladies' man,'' General Parks murmured for her
ear alone, his eyes twinkling. "Though you'd hardly credit
it by looking at him. Excellent address, you know. Has all
the old biddies eating out of his hand.''

Yes, Charly decided, despite appearances, Mr. Cranford
was also no foreigner to the art of dalliance. Perhaps the
allure of an accomplished older man, settled and respectable, might be just the thing for her flighty, romantic sister.

Yet when they went in to supper at midnight, Anthony
Martin was at Bella's side. Charly, squired by Jonathan
Treadwell, managed to be seated near enough to keep a

watchful eye on her sister and her bothersome partner. She could find nothing in his manners at which to cavil, for he neither put himself forward nor tried to monopolize Bella when others joined them. His behavior and address were all they should be. In fact, rather to Charly's annoyance, he appeared to be a friendly and likable boy.

But that was on the surface only, Charly reminded herself sternly. The glorious Mr. Anthony Martin was an admitted fortune hunter, and one who needed, for some obscure reason, to hide from his own brother!

If only Mr. Richard Cranford would indeed show an interest in Bella! An experienced man of the world must have tricks to fascinate a young lady that would overshadow Anthony Martin's blatant animal magnetism. She could only hope. On the whole, it was a very worried elder sister who finally tucked a glowing Bella into bed at four in the morning.

Not too many hours later, Charly gave up her attempts to recapture sleep after waking in the coils of a nightmare. Even in sleep, Mr. Anthony Martin allowed her no peace! In her dreams, he rode Summer Storm carrying her sister before him and leaping over monstrously high hedges and fences while she—not Bella!—screamed in terror.

The morning would be her own; Bella would sleep long and soundly. Nor would Aunt Augusta stir from her room until afternoon. The elderly lady had been far more weary than she would admit but, buoyed by her social triumph, she had retired full of plans for their next celebration. Isabella would be eighteen in another two weeks, and naturally that called for another grand ball. Charly smiled as she munched a piece of toast, peacefully alone in the breakfast room. Really, one could not tell who took the most pleasure in Bella's come-out, the girl herself or Miss Hanley.

As she sat at the table, taking her last bite, Jensen entered bearing a visiting card which he offered her on a salver.

"A Mr. Bentley has called, madam. He requests a few minutes of your time."

"My time? Whatever does he want with me?"

Jensen maintained a scrupulously blank expression, betraying curiosity only by the straying of his eyes to the name on the card. "I really could not say, Mistress Deane, but he specifically asked for you."

"Is he in the drawing room? Yes, tell him I will be with him at once." Charly looked at the card again: JNO. BENTLEY. She knew that name. In her mind a picture formed of a middle-aged gentleman encountered somewhere fairly recently... Of course—he was a friend of Jonathan Treadwell's. But what could he want with her? Well, the only way to find out would be to go down.

He rose as she entered, and bowed deeply. Charly curtsied in return, studying him with no little interest.

"Pray be seated," she said as she sat on the sofa.

He took a chair opposite her and pressed his fingertips together in a manner disturbingly reminiscent of Mr. Van Bleek.

"I will come directly to the point, ma'am," he began. "My friend, Mr. Treadwell, informs me that you wish to sell your racing stable as there will be a change in your circumstances." A thin smile, awkward in its obvious rarity, created new creases in his tight cheeks. "May I be among the first to wish you happy?"

Wrath welled within Charly's breast, and her cheeks flushed with the heat of her anger, giving way almost at once before an icy fury. She came to her feet, holding out her hand in dismissal. "Good day, sir. I regret that you have been misinformed. Believe me, I have neither the intention of selling Deane Farm nor the thought of remarriage."

Mr. Bentley stood hastily, taken aback by the force of her emotion. "If I have the matter wrong, ma'am, then I must apologize." Still he hesitated, as though not believing her.

Before Charly could reach the bell pull, Jensen appeared in the doorway as if by magic. "This way, sir," he intoned.

"Perhaps I am come too soon." Resignedly, Bentley walked to the door Jensen held open. "I only ask, ma'am, that you keep me in mind when you are ready to sell."

Charly stood rooted to the spot for a full minute after he left. Never had she been so angry with Jonathan. How dare he presume so much? And to bandy her name about in such a manner! Failing to control her temper after counting rapidly to five and twenty, she stormed upstairs to Augusta Hanley's bedroom. Bursting in unceremoniously, she caused that lady to spill several drops of her morning chocolate on her feather quilt.

"Good heavens, girl, what ails you at this ungodly hour?"

Charly plumped down on the end of the bed, further endangering both the chocolate and the comforter.

"I beg leave to tell you, Aunt Augusta, that your favorite has lost the field. He is rushing his fences in the most abominable manner and has just come a major cropper!"

"What on earth are you talking about?" Aunt Augusta mopped futilely with her napkin at the spreading stain on her bed. "For pity's sake, girl, do be more gentle, or I shall have to send poor Niddy for another cup."

Charly took a deep breath and smoothed back the tendrils of fair hair that always broke loose when she became agitated. "Your precious Jonathan, love. And this time I am really furious with him. Only think, he has sent me a purchaser for my farm, telling him I am to be married and will be giving up my stable!"

Augusta's face fell in comic dismay. "He couldn't have been so foolish!"

"He has. And what he hoped to gain by such a move, I cannot imagine!"

Her aunt straightened her disarranged quilt, a far easier task than smoothing Charly's temper. "I am sure he meant well, dearest. Though to display such a shocking lack of decorum! It is only that he knows, as I too believe, that sooner or later you must remarry. It is the only recourse for a female in dire financial straits. And he is by far the best—and wealthiest—choice."

"Best!"

"He knows of no rival, my dear. You cannot blame him if he continues to hope."

"He may put a period to any hope he still possesses! Why can he not take no for an answer?"

Augusta sighed and directed a searching look at her. "Charlotte, dear, perhaps you should reconsider. Do not burn all your bridges. You must know that if you wed again, it would mean the end of your problems."

"More like the beginning of them, you mean. I shall manage on my own, thank you."

This brought a slight frown to Augusta's wrinkled brow. "I fear you are fancying yourself a second Margaret Hardenbroeck, to carry on the business of your late husband and prosper as he never could."

Charly's scowl vanished and she almost laughed. Never one to retain her umbrage, she had begun to lose her anger at Jonathan once she had recited his wrongs. "Nay now, love." She smiled at her aunt. "I deal in horses, not in shipping, and I have no intention of going 'supercargo' on my own nags! Ben Stokes will ride in my races."

She got up, stretching, her good humor nearly restored. "Now, take off that Friday face. I must go and awaken Bella. We are due at an alfresco breakfast in less than an hour. Be good, dearest, and remain in bed today or I shan't allow you to give another ball for weeks!" She brushed a kiss on her aunt's cheek and went to pull the warm bedclothes off her slugabed sister.

The day was pleasant and sunny, and Bella appeared to be delighted by the novelty of the outdoor party. This was so, Charly noted with relief, even though Anthony Martin was not among those attending, and she had the pleasure of watching her sister walk cheerfully arm in arm with Mr. Richard Cranford.

The only blemish on her day came in the form of Jonathan Treadwell, who most injudiciously insisted on apologizing once again for pressing her so ardently while she was still in mourning.

"I came today particularly to seek you out," he told her left ear, since she refused to face him and acknowledge his presence. She had no intention of letting him off before giving herself the pleasure of ringing a rare peal over him.

"Only my desire to shield you from your difficulties led me to speak so harshly on the subject of your farm," he pleaded. "Do believe I have been cast into the greatest affliction by your disapproval. I have only your best welfare at heart.''

She rounded on him at this. ''And was it only your concern for my welfare that caused you to discuss me with Mr. Bentley? No doubt at the Tontine House over your wine cups! I'll thank you not to mention my name in public again! I consider it the greatest piece of impertinence.''

Treadwell blanched visibly. ''Bentley? But what—?''

''He came into my aunt's home under the impression that I was about to sell my farm and marry you! That will never happen, do you understand? Never!''

''Charlotte!'' He stared at her, aghast, his expression so pitifully stricken that she almost relented.

She softened her tone somewhat. ''Do try to get it clearly into your head, Jonathan, and not be such a goosecap. I will not sell and I will not remarry.''

She turned and walked away, but he followed, his abject apologies ringing in her ears. These were silenced only when they rejoined the rest of the party, who had adjourned to watch the lawn bowling. And there was Bella with the beautiful Anthony by her side, his eyes gleaming as they rested on her! So Bella knew he would be at the party all the time! No wonder she had been so excited and ready to enjoy herself.

A sense of desperation crept over Charly. Surely, by now he must have discovered their true financial situation. But what if that did not give him pause? Her lovely, lively little sister might constitute a prize worth his denying the world.

Charly could brook no connection with a fortune-hunting upstart on the run from his own brother for who knew what crime! She and Bella might be poor, but as Hanleys they were unquestionable members of New York's tight social circle, and they had their position to maintain. Bella must be blinded indeed by his handsome face if she thought that she, a young lady of rank and consequence, could find happiness with a penniless adventurer.

She watched Bella laughing up at the man, with her eyes glowing and a radiance about her face that Charly had never seen before. Bella was infatuated. And knowing her sister's volatile, impulsive nature, Charly's anxiety grew. Romantic

Bella. At the least sign of opposition, she was surely one to renounce all for love.

But that would never do for the girl! Bella needed stability, the stability that only money could bring. Mr. Richard Cranford was the perfect suitor, but it was not this estimable gentleman who brought that soft flush to Bella's lovely cheeks. How long would that glowing radiance last if she was forced to face life with a ne'er-do-well like Anthony Martin for a husband?

An excited, almost hysterical laugh from Bella caught Charly's attention. She glanced quickly at her sister, shocked to see dark circles beneath her eyes and feverish spots of color flaming in her cheeks. Oh, why hadn't she thought! Bella was unused to such late hours as she had been keeping. She was clearly exhausted and going on nerves alone. Charly rose at once and interrupted the game.

"Bella, dearest, we must go! It is late, and I wish to rest before evening."

Bella spun to face her, resentful and dismayed, clutching even tighter the bowling ball she had just retrieved. "Oh, Charly, no! It is barely past noon. I will not go!"

Anthony came to stand at her side, towering above her, smiling down with devastating effect. "Your sister is right, Miss Hanley. We none of us slept much this past night." His eyes held a lurking, teasing gleam as they rested on Bella. "We have another evening of pleasure ahead," he added, and his voice, soft and silky, worked magic.

Bella dropped the ball at once and raised her lovely face to look adoringly up at him. "Then we shall meet tonight at the Belmonts'?"

"Assuredly." He smiled again. Charly could never have achieved such instant compliance from Bella! Jealousy vied with her fear at the influence Anthony Martin already possessed over the girl.

He took one of Bella's hands. "Until tonight," he murmured, and the words were a calculated caress.

With no further protest, Bella accompanied a fuming Charly back to Aunt Augusta's house. Still in the bemused daze wrought solely by young Mr. Martin, she submitted meekly when her worried sister sent her up to lie down for a few hours. A small, happy smile hovered on her lips, a sure sign that her thoughts were far removed from the brick mansion on Beaver Street.

Charly, too concerned about her sister's preoccupation with the most unsuitable Mr. Martin to rest, paced up and down the length of the Aubusson carpet in the front parlor. Martin was a hardened flirt of obviously vast experience! What chance did the naive and innocent Bella have against him? And what could a worried elder sister do? Mr. Martin had already demonstrated the power he held.

She was still there, frowning over her reflections, when Jensen entered and announced Mr. Silas Hawkes. "He requests a word with you in private, madam."

Charly came to an abrupt halt behind the long sofa as she caught her breath in sudden fear. All other matters fled from her mind. Silas Hawkes, her nearest neighbor in the country, detested New York City! Nothing short of an emergency would bring him into town—an emergency, or a message from Ben Stokes.

Zephyr! Concern for her mare instantly replaced all else. Was she foaling? Her fingers whitened as she clutched the wooden trim along the back of the sofa. "Show him in, Jensen, at once!"

He was with her in moments, a solid-looking man in plain farmer's clothing that stood out at odd variance with the exquisite appointments of Augusta Hanley's parlor. He paused just inside the door, and something about his heavy stance confirmed Charly's fear.

"What is it, Mr. Hawkes? What has occurred? Is it Zephyr?" She ran to him and he took her agitated hands.

"Nay, now. 'Tis not the mare. She fares well."

He hesitated and Charly tried to calm herself. If not Zephyr, then . . . what?

With an obvious effort, he went on. "It's the stallion, ma'am. Summer Storm. Ben found him this morning, out in the back pasture."

A trembling began deep within her. She knew, just from his tone. There was no need to ask. Her horse was dead. "How . . . what happened?" she whispered.

Gently he led her to a chair and pressed her into it. Still

holding one of her hands and patting it, he seated himself beside her. His gruff voice sounded strangely muffled through the shock that engulfed her. "A stray bullet, we think, ma'am. One of those damned . . . I beg your pardon . . . one of those night hunters, I expect." He continued talking, giving her time. "Down in the Carolinas they made a law. It's a misdemeanor there to hunt deer at night because of the accidental slaughter of so many horses and cattle. That's what it must have been." He searched her stunned face anxiously. "We need a law like that here. Mebee we'll get one."

But it would be too late. Summer Storm—her stallion—was gone! Grief for her beloved horse gave way before an overpowering reality. All her hopes had been pinned on him. Even if Summer Wind won every race in New York City, without his great sire, Deane Farm had no future as an establishment for breeding.

CHAPTER
Four

"*I* happened by the lane and saw Ben and your two men digging him a grave back there where he fell."

Silas Hawkes's voice droned on as he gave Charly time to assimilate his news, to regain her composure. He was a kindly man, a good neighbor. He might be her greatest rival in breeding and on the racetrack, but there was no sign of triumph in him. He was honest, and would credit only a win by fair means, not one by a tragic accident such as this.

She forced herself to listen to his words and found that he, too, was offering to buy Deane Farm. He knew, almost as well as she, that the loss of Summer Storm meant the end for her.

"My own place adjoins, and I could use the land," he explained, his tone one of gentle persuasion. "By selling, you could bring yourself a tidy little fortune and live here in town quite comfortably."

Her weakening spine stiffened at these words. She would not give up without a fight! She might no longer have a stallion, but she would never part with the farm. She was made of sterner stuff than that. Her thoughts flew to Jonathan. How pleased he would be! And then they moved on to Van Bleek. He would foreclose on her the minute he heard—but he couldn't! She had the precious signed extension: she had six more months.

Somewhere, somehow, she would get another stud. Not one as good as Storm; that would be impossible. And not Summer Wind, for while he had the speed, he lacked his beautiful sire's conformation. But Zephyr was due to foal—a ray of hope! An offspring of Zephyr and Storm . . . now *there* might be a perfect animal. If only it was a colt, Deane Farm still had a chance. She was not defeated yet!

Before the end of her allotted time, if Summer Wind won all the races at the meet, her yearlings would sell for enough to pay off the remainder of the loan. At the very least, she must earn enough from them so that Pieter Van Bleek would grant her another extension.

Her only hope was Zephyr's foal, who with luck would possess the best qualities of each parent. Nothing must happen to the mare! The foal must be born safely. If hunters ranged at will in the hills behind Deane Farm . . .

Charly sprang to her feet, startling Silas Hawkes so that he broke off in mid-sentence.

"You must excuse me! I go to Deane Farm at once, to see that Ben posts a guard on Zephyr. She must not be let out into the pasture, and I shall have him bring all the horses in each night before dark."

Mr. Hawkes rose with her. "I'm going back now, ma'am. I could deliver your message for you, if you'd like."

"No. Oh, no. I want to go myself. I must see Ben and look after Zephyr." She broke off, then mastered the emotions that threatened to get the better of her. Extending her hand, she took his once again. "I . . . I cannot thank you enough for coming to me. It is so hard, I know, to be the one to break such news."

He shuffled his boots and looked down, embarrassed. "The least I could do, Mrs. Deane. Ben would have come, but he didn't want to leave the farm."

She blinked away the threat of tears. Quickly, before the reality became overpowering, she thanked Hawkes again and saw him to the door.

Still dazed, she closed it after him and turned, leaning her back against it for support. Ahead, she saw only disaster, financial ruin. The loss of Summer Storm could well mean the end of Deane Farm. She had put up a good front before Hawkes—after all, one did not break out in hysterical sobs before a guest—but inside she felt her foundation crumbling.

She was giving in! She shook herself and straightened up. Where was her backbone? All the determination and will to win she claimed to possess? She brushed back a few straying tendrils of hair that tickled her cheek.

Her aunt, upon learning the terrible news, stared at her in a combination of horror and relief. "You will have to marry Jonathan Treadwell, and at once!" she exclaimed. "Now, Charly, dearest, you must give way to reason. You have no other choice!"

"Then I will make one!" All at once she felt desperate to be away from her aunt's entreaties. It was no easy feat, but at last, almost half an hour later, she escaped.

Sending Jensen for her chaise, she ran up the stairs to change into a more suitable gown. This accomplished, she went to Bella's room, but hesitated in the doorway. The girl lay on her bed, breathing deeply and steadily. There would be time enough later to tell her what had occurred. The loss of Storm would break Bella's heart, for she had a genuine fondness for the horse. Her sister adored beauty, Charly thought grimly.

Once outside New York's crowded streets, she drove rapidly and soon topped a small hill. Below her stretched the lovely valley wherein lay Deane Farm, Silas Hawkes's spreading acres, and one other estate. Always, a sense of peace and well-being filled her each time she gazed down upon her stone and timber buildings, the broad green pastures with their zig-zag split rail fencing and the fruit orchard behind the house and barns. This time the sight brought a heart-wrenching fear. Was she about to lose it all?

She drew up by her gate, almost afraid to go farther. All looked so quiet, as if nothing had happened. For one wild moment, she wondered if Silas Hawkes had told her the truth. But he would have had no reason to tell such a tale unless it was true. He was no cruel jokester: her horse was gone, and it was no cover-up of a theft. Ben had carried out the burial.

As Bruno came to a halt, a gangly lad of fifteen ran out from the side barn to take charge of the chaise. His face was white and shocked.

"Thank you, Jim." She shook out her crumpled skirt. "Where is Mr. Stokes?"

"Out at back pasture, ma'am." Jim tugged at his forelock as Ben had taught him. "You do know, ma'am . . . Mr. Hawkes did tell you?"

Charly nodded.

"Shall I tell Mr. Stokes you've come, ma'am?"

"No, I'll find him." She walked past the house toward the paddock area, holding up her skirts and stepping cautiously around puddles left from rain the night before, conscious as she went of Jim's sympathetic eyes following her.

She kept a very small staff, a fact that by necessity bound them all closely together. Ben Stokes managed the outside area while his wife, Myra, cooked and kept house for Charly and Bella. Jim, quick in both thought and action, exercised those horses not directly in Ben Stokes's care. The other lad, Henry, was solid and muscular, a year older than Jim but mentally not his equal. Henry mucked out the stables and did general cleanup.

Everything looked so ordinary, so familiar, yet it had all changed. No longer would Summer Storm whinny at the mares or kick irritably at his stall door when his oats were late in coming. It would be so strange without him. All on the farm had revolved about the stallion, all but Zephyr and her coming foal. Clinging to this remaining bit of her existence, Charly ran headlong toward Zephyr's paddock.

The mare saw her coming and thrust her head over the fence, snuffling and whickering. Charly flung her arms about the horse, burying her face in the warm neck and tangling her fingers in the flowing mane. At last, pent-up tears coursed down her cheeks.

Here was her friend, her solace . . . Beyond reason, she hugged the mare, whispering broken, sobbing phrases into pointed ears that knew not her words but seemed to understand the feeling behind them. Bella, Summer Storm, their lack of money, her aloneness in a world full of people—all Charly's worries came tumbling out, to be replaced by the

solid, warm presence of her Zephyr, the one hope in her
crashing world. Gradually, her shattered spirits began to
rebuild. She was almost herself again when she heard
footsteps behind her and turned to see Ben Stokes.

He joined her by the fence and spat out the straw he had
been chewing. "Won't be long now, Mrs. Deane." He
reached out and rubbed on Zephyr's withers. A small man,
he had extraordinarily strong hands and a prematurely lined
face, made of wire and leather, Charly often thought. There
wasn't much he didn't know about horses.

"I give her a week, maybe less," he added.

Charly surreptitiously wiped at her tear-stained cheeks.
"We'd best keep her in." By silent agreement, neither
mentioned Summer Storm or what his loss meant to Deane
Farm.

"Aye." Ben glanced at her for a moment and quickly
looked away. "If you'll excuse me, Mrs. Deane, I'll be
about my work."

Charly nodded, knowing that behind his words there was
both concern and a wish to give her privacy. He walked
away and she slipped under the rail to stand beside Zephyr.
She put her arms around the mare's neck, ignoring the horse
hair that rapidly sullied the front of her gray merino traveling gown. Zephyr stood quietly as she combed the mare's
mane with her fingers while she struggled to regain her
composure.

Bella's voice, high and excited, startled her from her
reverie. She looked up, and her heart sank. Anthony Martin
followed her sister down the path.

"Charly! Oh, Charly, I had to be with you, as soon as
Aunt Augusta told me! And then Tony came by. I asked him
to bring me to the farm at once." Bella's words tumbled out
in her anxiety to explain. She ran over, grasping her sister's
hands over the rail fence and giving them a tight, comforting
squeeze. There was no need for either to voice their sorrow.

"Tony had borrowed a carriage from the Binghams to
take me for a drive. Was it not fortunate? I suggested at
once that we come here!"

"Who else is with you?" Charlotte was suddenly alert to

the danger to Bella's reputation. "Is there a groom, or did Aunt Augusta send a maid?"

"Oh, no." Bella stared at her blankly. "We came alone."

"I see." Charly breathed heavily, and her words held a wealth of meaning. To have driven out of town in the company of a single gentleman was a shocking indiscretion. Charly knew she should take her sister to task, but she could not fault her for flying to her side. Instead, she contented herself with being icily polite to the gentleman who caused the dilemma.

"I must thank you, sir." She raised a haughty eyebrow as he turned away to look at her horse. "And was Miss Hanley's Aunt Augusta not up to coming with you?" she asked in pointed concern. "Or could she not spare Miss Nidbury?"

"Oh!" Bella, suddenly conscious of the impropriety of her actions, shot a dismayed glance at Martin. He seemed not to have heard the exchange, for he had gone to the other side of the paddock to stroke Zephyr. "Oh, Charly, truly I did not think! I will never do it again."

Charly sighed. "Does our aunt know where you've gone?"

"Oh, yes." Bella sounded relieved. "She was sleeping, so I left her a note."

"I say." Martin came back to them, all smiling charm. "I wonder if I may see some of the other wondrous horses Bella . . . Miss Hanley . . . has told me about? I understand you are racing one soon. This mare is a beauty. Are the others out in the back fields?"

Charly had no desire to extend him her friendship, but showing off her horses just a bit was a temptation she could never resist. She began to lead the way to the pastures. Anthony Martin walked beside them, talking cheerfully. Did he know about Storm? she wondered. Of course, he must. He had just driven out in the company of Bella, the human newspaper. Reluctantly she gave him credit for being very circumspect.

"My brother has a stud farm in Ireland," he informed them. "He has some land there left us by an uncle, where he breeds thoroughbreds."

"Charly's mares are Arabian. She's crossing them

with . . . with a thoroughbred." Bella's voice stumbled, avoiding Storm's name. "To get racing stock, you know."

They had come to the yearlings' pasture, and Martin leaned on the fence as Mr. Marlowe had done, enraptured, watching the colts and fillies at play. Beyond the fence, in the next field, were Charly's other mares.

"My brother has a few well-bred mares, only none have the looks of these!" he admitted admiringly. "But he has a stallion! Excalibur, he calls it. You should see him, Mrs. Deane."

Charly accorded this a polite smile. "If ever I get to Ireland, I shall certainly look him up."

Martin grinned. "You wouldn't like him. He's a pompous stuffed shirt. Oh, you meant you'd look up Excalibur!" The young man laughed, an easy, infectious sound. "Now, that horse is a marvel. I ride him, you must know, and we win every steeplechase we enter! He has perfect manners, and would you believe it? Every one of his foals takes after him. My brother's absolutely mad about that horse. You know, when I heard he was in this country looking for me, I was amazed. I never thought he'd be parted from the animal for so long!"

"You say you race him, not your brother?"

"Oh, he rides much too heavy for racing."

"I see." Charly glanced at his handsome profile. "And have you a favorite horse of your own?"

"No, I've no need," he replied carelessly. "I ride my brother's whenever I please. And in all the races, of course. That's probably one reason he's come after me."

Charly's delicate eyebrows rose. "And have you run away to America to make your fortune, Mr. Martin?"

His charming smile flashed. "But of course. Does not every Englishman's younger son? Someday I hope to own my own land."

Oh, do you indeed? Charly thought savagely. Well, it won't be *my* land. She looked back for Bella, who had lagged behind, picking her way daintily among the ruts and puddles.

"My brother races sometimes," Martin rambled on. "Two years ago he took a header over a regular rasper and broke his arm. There he was, in what must have been agony, and all he could think of was his horse's knees. Wouldn't leave the field until they assured him that his nag was all right." He shook his head, still smiling at what to him seemed eccentric behavior. "He's schooling one of Excalibur's colts," he went on. "You know, they've started racing two-year-olds in England now, on the flat."

"Oh, like our Hempstead Plains," put in Bella, who had caught up. "Summer Wind is going to run there someday. Can we show him to T . . . Mr. Martin, Charly?"

Charlotte bit her lower lip gently. Really, she was going to have to talk with Bella about using a young man's first name, and the sooner the better. "This way, Mr. Martin," she said curtly emphasizing the surname.

Summer Wind cantered along the fence as they walked up, his head and tail both high, his hooves barely touching the ground. Martin whistled, impressed.

"Wouldn't I like to ride that horse!" he exclaimed. "Do you have a jockey for your race?"

Bella danced up, clapping her hands. "Oh, Charly, do let him! He could win for us, for he wins all the time at home."

Charlotte shook her head, not at all pleased. "Ben will ride him. He knows him and can handle him."

"Tony could do it!" In her disappointment, Bella forgot herself and used his first name in a way that seemed so natural that it was obvious to Charly that their friendship had deepened more quickly than she could have believed possible.

"No," she said flatly. Then, realizing how impolite it sounded, she turned to the young man. "He is somewhat temperamental, and takes considerable handling. I am sure you know how that is." Neatly, she changed the subject. "Do you school the horses as well as ride?"

"My brother does that. He has the muscle and the patience for all the hard work."

Unlike you, Charly thought. Your brother works and you show off the results and earn all the glory. In a way, he was like Bella, she admitted to herself ruefully. For weeks she had been ripping seams, cutting fabric, and sewing to create a glory for her sister from the voluminous skirts of her old ball gowns so that Bella could have a triumphant season in society. But Bella was grateful and appreciative, while this Tony seemed very casual in his attitude toward his brother. And why was he hiding from him? There was some mystery there, and she could not like it.

Summer Wind flung up his beautiful head and turned, cantering with a long, easy stride toward the fence that separated him from the mare's pasture. Charly, remembering another stallion running free, turned away abruptly. Suddenly she needed quiet. To lose Summer Storm and then have to show an unwelcome visitor over her farm was too much.

Later, after she had sent Bella and Martin, with Myra Stokes as chaperon, back to New York, she asked Ben to show her where Summer Storm had been buried. They stood in silence for a while by the mound of freshly turned earth that lay in the far corner of the field, at the base of a little hillock just inside her back fence.

"I wonder if he even knows what he did?" she mused at last.

"Who, Mrs. Deane?"

"The hunter. Mr. Hawkes told me it was a stray bullet. Whoever made that shot in the dark may have been too far away to have known he hit him."

Ben frowned. "Mr. Hawkes told you it was a hunter, ma'am?" He shook his head. "Whatever would he tell you such a thing for? It was no stray bullet. Storm was shot neat and clean, behind the left ear, by someone standing right beside him. Mrs. Deane, that horse was killed deliberate."

CHAPTER

Five

*C*harly stared at Ben, trying to assimilate his words. It wasn't—couldn't be—true! Summer Storm deliberately killed? She shook her head, not wanting to believe the implications.

"Ben, are . . . are you sure? You can't be! It's impossible. You must have imagined it!"

Ben stood his ground. "Sorry, Mrs. Deane. I saw the powder burns. No mistake about them."

"But . . . but why?" Her thoughts raced in chaos. To ruin her? To end her breeding program? Or cause her to lose her farm? But who would do such a terrible thing?

Blindly she looked out across the pasture, toward the raw patch of newly turned soil. Who? Who knew the importance of Storm, both to the success of her business and to the continuance of her breeding program? And who would go to such desperate, despicable means to stop it, to ruin her? Another breeder?

She could think of only one who had already developed a speed in his horses capable of challenging the supremacy of her blood line: Silas Hawkes. But he was a friend! Their rivalry on the track had always been friendly. Only now . . . Her heart gave an uncomfortable lurch as she remembered his offer to buy her land. She had thought it merely a kind gesture, to buy her out as a measure to save her from financial disaster. His place might be a little small, but he had no real need for her acres—or so she had thought. But what if . . . no! Silas Hawkes wouldn't. She simply could not believe it. There was nothing either crooked or cruel about the man. He would not have done it. But how could anyone?

Her eyes widened but remained unfocused. Yes, *how* could anyone have done it? Slowly she turned back to Ben. "Was it someone he knew?" She asked the thought that puzzled her. "A stranger could never have gotten so close to him! Storm was never a friendly horse."

Ben picked a blade of grass and began to chew on it. "Mebee not, but he'd come to anyone offering an apple. Found him out there, just inside the back fence. The lane's just beyond."

Charlotte ran a distraught hand over her forehead. "But Mr. Hawkes told me . . . why would he tell me it was a hunter . . . a stray bullet? He was there when you buried him; he must have known!" Even as she spoke, she realized why. Silas Hawkes was an old-fashioned man with firm ideas on the delicacy of females. He probably feared she'd faint or have hysterics if he told her the truth. Well, he wasn't far wrong! She tried to think calm and settling thoughts. About what—Storm's killer? Zephyr about to foal? Bella and her infatuation with the impossible Mr. Martin.

"Not much else to say." Ben spat out the blade of well-chewed grass. "Just what you've already heard. Saw him lying out there when I came out this morning. Knew something was wrong because I carried his bucket of oats and he was always waiting at the gate for it. After I saw him, I called the boys and we started digging him a grave where he lay. No way we could move him. Mr. Hawkes came driving down the lane and saw us, so he stopped and helped. Said he had business in town and he'd take word to you. Where he got that stray bullet idea, I don't know. Saw as well as I did what really happened."

Charly nodded. "He . . . he no doubt cloaked the truth, hoping to save me worry." But worry, she did!

Well before dark, Charly watched as Jim and Henry brought the horses in from the pastures, leading each to a carefully prepared loose box. Zephyr munched her hay contentedly, showing none of the restlessness common in a mare about to foal. Nevertheless, Charly was not happy to have to leave.

That evening Charly and Bella were pledged to attend a drum. The company was lively and Charly hoped that if she retired to a corner among the chaperons, no one would notice that she herself took no part. Therefore, as soon as she had seen Bella safely established in a group that included a smiling Richard Cranford, she slipped into a chair in the farthest corner of the drawing room, where she was mostly hidden by a potted palm.

To her dismay, she soon found herself reviewing the name of every man she knew, with suspicion uppermost in her mind. Most could have no motive at all for killing Storm; these she dismissed. But Hawkes? Every part of her rebelled against the idea. He was a friend, as she had had ample proof over the past years. Pieter Van Bleek? He was a city man. Surely he would rather see her succeed so that he would receive his money rather than having to foreclose on land outside of town. Jonathan Treadwell? Absurd! He hadn't the gumption. Other men she knew had racehorses, but surely it would be Summer Wind, their competition, they'd wish out of the way, not his aging sire.

Throughout the party, Charly's sense of unease grew. Try as she might, she could not shake it off. And then Jonathan, a late arrival, discovered her hiding place and bore down upon her, still bent on winning her forgiveness for prompting Mr. Bentley's unfortunate visit.

"My dear Charlotte, I most humbly beg your pardon," he declared as he drew up a chair beside hers. "I cannot see how he became convinced that you were about to sell Deane Farm. I swear I never told the man any such thing!"

"You must have told him something," she snapped, wishing that he would leave her alone. His presence only increased her perturbation.

"No, I promise you. But I fear my attentions toward you have been noted and my sentiments must be obvious to all. I shall never forgive myself if my concern for you has made you the object of unwelcome gossip."

"Oh, please. Do cut line, Jonathan. It is no great thing,

after all," she exclaimed, exasperated beyond endurance by his entreaties. "I believe I disabused Mr. Bentley of his odd notions." Now, if only she could disabuse Treadwell of his, as well! She turned away from him and began pointedly to talk to her nearest neighbor, Anabel Brougham, a doughty spinster who was a bosom bow of her aunt.

This proved almost as difficult to bear, for that lady had a pronounced turn for the romantic. Her sharp eyes had not failed to notice the incredibly beautiful Mr. Anthony Martin, who now stood at Bella's side, in complete possession of the field. Surely, Miss Brougham marveled, he cast all rivals in the shade! No one, she was sure, could compare with his manners and appearance. How delighted her dear Charlotte must be to see so fine a gentleman honoring her little sister with such flattering attention.

What Charly really thought, she was mercifully able to keep to herself. The music started, and Martin led Bella into a set that was forming. The picture the two made as they whirled and curtsied and bowed sent Miss Brougham into raptures and Charly into a furious despair.

"Did you ever see such a pair!" Miss Brougham declared. "So perfectly matched, him so dark and she fair as a princess." The lady sighed deeply. "You must be that proud of your lovely little sister, Charlotte." She lowered her voice suggestively and hid their faces behind her fan. "Tell me now, are we not soon to receive a most delightful announcement?"

Charlotte stared at her, startled and revolted. "Good God, no!" she exclaimed, far too loudly. Several heads turned her way and she flushed. "I mean, Isabella is not yet eighteen, remember. I could hardly countenance . . . or welcome! . . . a serious attachment with one who is, after all, a stranger to our town!"

"Very true." Disappointed, Miss Brougham agreed, though it was clear that she, at least, felt that extreme youth should not be a bar to such blissful happiness as these two must obviously find together.

The brief exchange left Charlotte shaken. If all the *haut ton* of New York shared Anabel Brougham's surmise, it made the situation more desperate than she had previously viewed it. Once Bella's name was linked to Tony Martin's in gossip, the girl's reputation would hang in the balance. Marriage, to anyone, would be the only recourse. And Charlotte longed for Bella to take her time, to meet a number of young men, to have the luxury that she herself had been denied, of selecting her own perfect husband.

Not much to her surprise, she found she had lost all interest in the party. Instead she watched Bella's every move, noting with whom she talked, and which gentleman brought the lovely, lilting laugh to her lips. It soon dawned on her that this came less often than usual. Bella, too, did not seem her normal self, being disturbed and taking little pleasure in an event that normally would have sent her into raptures.

When the next dance ended, the girl abandoned her partner and, to Charly's dismay, went in search of Martin. Too restless to remain seated, Charly rose and paced about the floor.

Bella, seeing her sister's agitation, grabbed Tony Martin by the hand and came running up to her.

"Charly, we have come up with the most marvelous scheme! Tony has offered to drive us back to the farm tonight. Do let us go! I know how worried you are. Tony says you will feel so much better if you are there, and I am sure he is right!"

So the delightful and conniving young Martin was trying to ingratiate himself with her, was he? Well, it would not fadge. He would learn very quickly he had taken the wrong sow by the ear, to use a rather unflattering comparison. But going home to the farm . . . Suddenly the prospect held an overwhelming—no, irresistible!—appeal. It was the only thing she wanted to do. She would certainly know no rest in town. Besides, she had the excuse of needing to return Myra Stokes to the farm.

Restraining her eagerness, she turned a repressive eye on the source of this welcome suggestion. "Thank you, Mr. Martin. It is most considerate in you, I am sure, to offer. But we will not trespass upon your kindness. There is a full moon tonight and the road is in fair condition even though it has rained. Bella, if you will accompany me, let us leave this party at once."

She directed a dismissive nod to Tony and encountered an appreciative gleam in his eyes. The point went to her, this time, but she did not trust the Beautiful Tony one inch. Unless she was careful, it would be he who would lead her sister away on the next occasion.

Bella, surprised and more than a little disappointed, threw a wistful glance at Tony's handsome face. She made no demur, however, when Charly gathered their things and made their excuses to their hostess.

While to Bella the idea appeared to be a perfectly natural one, Aunt Augusta was horrified when they returned at an unseasonable hour and announced they were leaving the city at once.

"You cannot!" She bundled her dressing gown more closely about her slight frame as she sat upright in her bed. "Have you taken leave of your senses?"

"I cannot stay, dearest," Charly said coaxingly, trying to soothe her. "I am too worried to sleep so far from home. Surely you can see that. I must be there to be certain all is well. If anything should happen, it would be hours before Ben or Mr. Hawkes could bring me word."

"Your mare." Miss Hanley plucked at her quilt, disgusted. "All you think of is that animal these days. Surely she can foal without you holding her . . . her hoof."

Charly managed a laugh, but her conviction grew that if she was not at the farm something would go amiss.

As soon as they had changed from their ball gowns into warm traveling dresses, she sent for Bruno and her chaise. Thankful for the moon and a clear night, Charly drove the horse with a sense of urgency, almost recklessly, in the near darkness. The feeling that something was about to happen spurred her on, and they reached Deane Farm in record time.

All was calm there, and Ben Stokes stumbled out of his cottage in nightshirt and breeches, surprised but not unduly disturbed to see them. "Reckoned you'd take some such notion into your head, Mrs. Deane," he said sleepily as he took charge of their turnout. "Though I'm pleased to see my missus."

After a quick visit to Zephyr's box, where they found the mare peacefully lipping hay, Charlotte and Bella retired to their rooms. Donning a linen nightdress, Charly braided her long fair hair and slipped between the sheets. But even here, at the farm, sleep proved elusive. After spending considerable time in fruitless tossing, she rose and went to the window, where she stood staring out over the moonlit stables.

Over and over, her thoughts returned to Summer Storm. Who would do such a thing? How could anyone end the life of so strong and beautiful an animal purely for material gain—if that was the reason? But what was there that someone could have gained by it? How did injuring her profit anyone? She felt totally at a loss.

She gripped the window sill, suddenly alert. Was that a light? It flashed again and was quickly doused as though someone walked between the barns with a lantern. Without a second thought, she caught up a shawl and ran down the stairs. Familiar with every rut and obstacle, she needed no light. And she wasn't alone. Ben slept in his small cottage by the second barn, while Jim and Henry shared the groom's quarters above the carriage house. She had only to shout to bring them to the scene.

And perhaps it was one of them whom she chased. Could Zephyr be foaling? She ran faster. As she passed the first barn, she heard the sound of someone falling over a bucket followed by a stifled curse. Not from Zephyr's loose box—it came from farther along, where Summer Wind was stalled for the night.

Fear for the horse gripped her. If something happened to him before the race . . . His winning, and proving the worth of her other colts by Storm, was her last hope!

"Ben?" she called softly in a quavering voice. "Ben, is that you?"

Suddenly the silence around her took on an ominous feeling. Nothing stirred; all seemed held in suspense, waiting. A louder cry could bring everyone, but not before the intruder had a chance to escape. Finding out who wanted to ruin her was almost as important as saving Wind at the moment. Until that person was uncovered, he would keep trying—until he succeeded.

Feeling along the barn wall for a weapon, she armed herself with the first that came to hand: a pitchfork. She crept forward, trembling but determined, stepping silently in her bare feet—until she tripped over the bucket already kicked into the path by the clumsy intruder. It clattered against the stone wall of the barn. Charly staggered to retain her balance—and someone dashed past her and out of the yard.

"Ben!" she screamed. "Ben, catch him!" Too late, of course. Why had she been such a fool? She should have called Ben first instead of trying her own heroics! Had she really expected to discover her foe's identity?

Ben burst from the door of his cottage between the barns, his nightshirt pale in the moonlight, holding up his breeches with one hand as he ran.

"That way!" Charly shouted at him. "He must be running out the gate!" But whoever it was had a horse waiting. They heard the pounding of hooves before they could clear the buildings.

Charly stopped and sagged against the wall of the front barn. "He's gone."

Ben hefted the musket he carried, and pulled down his nightcap that had slipped askew. "We'd best check the horses, ma'am." He sounded grim. "I'll fetch a lantern."

As he spoke, Jim ran up, followed by Henry. "I saw him!" Jim exclaimed. "I looked out the window when Mrs. Deane yelled and from up there I saw someone runnin' in the moonlight. He had a horse out in the lane under the elm tree!" He held up a dark lantern. "Didn't have time to light it."

Ben dispatched Henry to fetch two more lanterns from his cottage and turned to Charly, who was already looking over Zephyr inch by inch. "Ma'am, the boys and me will look. You get back in and put on some boots and . . . er . . . other things."

"She's all right. See to Wind. I heard *him* near Wind's box."

Suddenly weak with reaction, she put a hand against the wall. As soon as her knees stopped wobbling, she would go in. Ben, she noted, had not told her to stay inside, merely to don proper clothes. Only Henry had pulled on footgear, and he wore one boot and one galosh. Had she not been so frightened, she would have enjoyed the sight of the ill-assorted group. Tomorrow, if all was well, she would remember Ben's tasseled cap and the way Jim had tucked only one side of his nightshirt into his breeches and maybe she'd smile. These thoughts steadied her and she hurried inside, where she pulled a cloak over her nightgown and put her bare feet into her boots.

They were already returning when she came back out of the house. Three lanterns bobbed along the path between the rows of paddocks, and the voices that reached her were calm and reassuring.

"All's well, ma'am." Ben met her by the barn. "He must have just come, and I don't see what game he was planning on. No sign of any damage, but I'm going to stay up and keep watch while the boys get some sleep. Then I'll put Jim on for the rest of the night."

"Wind is . . . is all right?"

"He's fine, ma'am. You go back to bed. The boys and me will keep guard."

Charly had to look at Summer Wind herself before she went back to bed as ordered. She did not sleep.

Early morning found her in the kitchen by the fireplace, drinking coffee from a large mug. Bella must have slept through the night's commotion, for her bedroom lay at the front of the house, overlooking the lane. For a fleeting moment, Charly envied her. She did not relish the job of telling her sister of their prowler.

When Bella at last came down for breakfast, she was every bit as shocked as Charly had feared. Her exclamations were not, though, for the safety of their animals or even themselves. "Oh, Charly, why did you not call me?" she exclaimed, indignant. "I could have helped!"

Charlotte smiled, though a bit wearily. "Doing what, love? Moral support? No, with Ben and the boys alert and on the watch, there is very little we can do. I shall stay, however, but there is no need for you to do so. You must go back to New York, for you have many engagements."

"I most certainly will not! A fine thing it would be if I placed my parties above your horses! No, I shall stay here and help you. You need me!" Bella informed her stoutly, albeit with a wistful note in her voice. "There is only the Ridgeways' rout tomorrow night and then . . ."

"And you shall go to it, Bella, and to all the others as well," Charlotte vowed, touched by her sister's determination to forego the parties she had dreamed of for more than a year. "You may stay today, but I promise you shall be back in New York tomorrow."

Bella accepted with alacrity and promptly set about making the best use of her time at the farm.

"You say you fell over a bucket and made a tremendous racket," she said musingly. "Charly, that is what we must do! Let us set up traps all over the yard, before the entry to each stall—tubs of water, pots and pans rigged to fall and clatter if someone walks into a rope across the doors. Oh, Charly, it will be fun! I mean, we must keep anyone from getting near the horses!" she added hastily.

Bella's day sped by in an almost enjoyable fashion. Had the stakes not been so high, Charlotte would have been highly entertained by her elaborate schemes. The girl enlisted Jim and Henry, both of whom were young enough to enter into her project with enthusiasm. Henry suggested a school-boy trick, balancing a pail of water over each door.

"Nay, now!" Jim protested. "We need noise, not just a quiet dousing! There's old cowbells in the barn. Why don't we use those?"

Bella clapped her hands. "A capital idea, Jim!"

An exhaustive search turned up the set of ancient cowbells, and these they hung on the doors of the barn where Summer Wind had his box. Jim stiffened the hinges with splinters of wood, and the jerk now required to pull them open would set the bells clanging. There were not enough bells to go around, so precarious piles of buckets, pitchers, and tin cups were set in front of the second barn. Farm implements were dragged to block pathways and hay nets were strung between the barns. Their combined ingenuity created some formidable obstacles to anyone moving about in the dark.

Lastly, they moved Zephyr to the small third barn, which was not rigged with noisemakers, for Charly did not want her disturbed should any commotion take place in the night.

Jim and Henry offered to stand the first guard. Ben declared he would sleep with his musket loaded and at the ready by his bed.

Toward evening, a rider cantered down their lane. Anthony Martin. Charly, who was still dressed in the late Abner's buckskin breeches and jerkin that constituted her stable clothes, was in no mood for guests. She greeted him with considerable reserve, at the same time grudgingly giving him full credit for manners in the way he ignored her unorthodox dress as he gallantly bent to kiss her hand. Bella, however, plainly delighted to see him, poured out the tale of the previous night's happenings and carried him off proudly to see all their traps. Charly could hear his shouts of laughter as she hurried in to change into a gown and brush her hair.

When she came back, she discovered the two of them just outside the back entrance, sitting on the ground and chuckling over something they were devising that seemed to involve a large pot of molasses and the box of chicken feathers Mrs. Stokes had cleaned for a pillow.

"Oh, Charly!" Bella bounced up, smoothing down her skirt. "Only wait till you see! Tony has thought of the most wonderful trap."

He rose also, dusting his breeches, and sketched an apologetic bow. "Mrs. Deane, I hope you do not mind."

"That depends." Charly came over and looked into the bucket they were filling. "Whatever are you up to?"

"It's quite simple, ma'am." Martin bent, eager to explain. "The feathers must come out last, you see, so we put them in the bucket first. Then we put the tin plate on top, and pour in the molasses. We put the bucket over the door of the stall where Summer Wind is housed. When the door is opened, the pail will be knocked from where it's balanced on the front edge. Our victim is first coated with the molasses and then feathered! That should discourage him from any further harassment!" He beamed at her, suddenly seeming no older than Jim or Henry.

Bella thought him wonderful. "Isn't it the most delightful idea, Charly? Tony planned it all!" Her eyes sparkled with pleasure and admiration for the superior mind that could devise anything so devilish. "Do say we may set it in place!"

Charly looked at her glowing face, and hadn't the heart to refuse. Bella, at least, was happy and enjoying herself. "Yes." She nodded. "But be sure you tell Ben and the boys. We don't want one of them to be caught when they go out to feed the horses this evening."

While they completed their preparations, Charly wandered to the paddock entrance, stepping carefully to miss the mud-filled ruts in the pathway. It had rained again, just before dawn, a fine misting drizzle, and there was more in the offing if she was any judge of the matter. She made a mental note to have one of the boys shovel in more dirt and gravel, for one puddle just inside the gate bade fair to become a small lake. She was contemplating it when the "children," as she had come to term them, came up to her, Tony striding freely and Bella skipping gaily by his side.

"Oh, we must not let this go to waste!" The young man stopped at the edge of the large muddy puddle. "It is a perfect place for a trip wire to stop the most eager intruder! Have you a length of rope that will reach from one post to the other?"

Bella ran off to find Ben and soon returned with a neatly coiled hank of hempen line. In minutes, Tony had affixed it to the two posts, stringing it tightly about one foot above the ground. He stepped back to admire his handywork. "There. Anyone attempting to come through here in the dark will get a soaking!"

Charlotte shook her head. "It's no doubt a fine idea, but take it down for now. We cannot endanger everyone who may come in. We can put it up again, the last thing before we all retire."

Bella had been eyeing the puddle critically. "Do you think it is deep enough? We could fill pails at the trough by the barn and make it into quite a lake."

Charlotte gave up. Leaving them to it, she went inside. Jim and Henry could fill in their pond in the morning. Meanwhile, dinner time was rapidly approaching, for they kept country hours at Deane Farm and she had best warn Myra. From her vast experience with her little sister, she had not a doubt that Bella would invite Anthony Martin to join them for the meal. She would have little choice but to second the invitation.

Why, she wondered, did he persist in charming Bella? He must know by now on what shaky financial ground they stood. Bella was no prize for a fortune hunter!

Perhaps he considered their difficulties a new form of sport and wanted to play a part. Or maybe he had another purpose, such as the coming race meet. He had already said how much he wanted to ride Wind in this. That was undoubtedly the answer, and his intent was to ingratiate himself to the point where she would permit it. Well, he was mistaken. From what little she had seen of him, she suspected that he was thoroughly spoiled and would go to any lengths to get whatever he wanted.

It was late when they finally sat down to dine. To Charlotte's surprise, they talked long, and mostly about horses. Tony Martin was full of tales of his brother, whom he clearly idolized, and his wonderful stallion, Excalibur. He made no mention of why he hid from him now, and Charlotte, succumbing to curiosity, finally asked him outright.

His answer, to her dismay, proved evasive. "Oh, the old boy has concocted a scheme I want no part of," he said airily. "He'll get over it eventually, and meanwhile I've only to keep out of his way."

No doubt that was how he avoided all responsibility, Charly thought, watching his carelessly cheerful face as he entertained Bella with yet another story. She would be glad when Martin's brother finally found him. Once such a toplofty and straitlaced gentleman as Tony described knew how the land lay, he would help her detach his young brother from Bella with all speed. In the meantime, there seemed little she could do other than maintain a distant politeness and not show the opposition that would cause Bella to fancy herself a Juliet.

Kevin Marlowe partook of his own meal in the dining parlor of the four-story brick Tontine Coffee House, where he had taken up temporary residence while he sought to locate his elusive brother. Recommended by Van Bleek as having the finest accommodations, with board and lodging for ten shillings a day, it also served as the chief gathering place for local businessmen.

After several days of fruitless inquiring at what must have been most of the over one thousand inns in New York City, he had as yet found no trace of Anthony Marlowe. Finding one young man in a town of over sixty thousand people proved to be no easy task.

His visit to the Binghams on his first evening had not been productive. Or had it? He pushed his emptied plate back and sipped from the glass of excellent port the inn provided. The Binghams admitted to a son named George who had brought home with him a young guest, but not one named Marlowe. George usually entertained a friend or two on his infrequent visits, they said. He was not now at home to be questioned, having been sent on a duty-visit to his grandfather in Philadelphia. The guest? He had not accompanied George, electing to remain in New York. He had, so he said, seen a most ravishing girl in the street outside the library and was determined to make her acquaintance at any cost. The more Kevin thought about it, the more certain he became that the "Mr. Martin" described by the Binghams had to be his brother Anthony. His chair scraped as he shoved it from the table. It was early yet. The Binghams were about to receive a second visit.

Less than an hour later, having secured his phaeton and team from the livery stable on Wall Street where he'd housed them, Kevin Marlowe was once more on his way to Deane Farm. Young Mr. Martin, the elder Bingham had informed him, had attended a ball with them several nights before and found his lovely lady. All day he had been full of her charms. No, they did not know her, she was not a resident of New York, merely visiting with her aunt, who was an old friend of theirs. Mr. Martin had told them the girl lived not far out of town with her sister, a widow who conducted a racing stable. Kevin had a premonition. Not Deane farm? Why, yes. Did he then know of the family? Grimly, he assured them he did, and headed for the livery stable. The damage to the phaeton that had necessitated his rental of the straight-pasterned roan on his arrival had finally been repaired and he was once more in command of his own equipage. Dusk already, he noted. It would be dark when he reached the farm, but this interview with those fortune-hunting females could not be delayed. He'd pry Anthony from their clutches before another day passed. The Deane woman would not pay off her mortgage with his money!

At Deane Farm, Charly still brooded, unhappy over the easy terms on which the young couple continued. When she went out to take one last look at Zephyr, they accompanied her while Ben, who was on guard duty, went to fetch Martin's horse for him. The moon had not yet risen, and Charly carried a lantern. The rest of the farm lay in peaceful darkness.

They had just closed Zephyr's stall door, Martin and Bella resetting a pail full of old horseshoes they had balanced on top of it, when they were startled by a commotion at the farm entrance—a shattering splash followed by a spate of words Charly had never before heard.

"Good God," Tony cried. "We forgot to take down the trip line!" He set off at a run with Charly in pursuit and Bella picking her delicate way along in the dark behind.

Ben Stokes was there before them, holding a lantern high in one hand, the other keeping his musket trained on a dripping, muddied, and thoroughly furious gentleman.

Charly stared in horror at the rough-hewn features reflected in the lantern light—the unforgettable features of Mr. Kevin Marlowe.

Beside her, Martin went off into howls of uncontrollable laughter. "Kev!" he finally managed to say between gasps for breath. "It's my brother Kevin!"

CHAPTER

Six

*M*r. Kevin Marlowe drew himself up to his fullest height, a proceeding made rather difficult by the unsteady slipping of his booted feet in the muddy puddle. Squinting, he peered into the darkness beyond the wavering circle of light that fell over him from an ancient lantern. The shadowy figure who held this also held, incongruously, an equally wavering musket. The barrel glinted in the dim glow—and seemed to be pointing directly at him. Kevin mopped dirty water from his face with a mud-soaked coat cuff and looked again.

Running feet approached, and a voice he knew only too well shouted his name. "Kev! It's my brother Kevin!" And the damnable young idiot went off into howls of infuriating laughter!

"Oh, sir!" A horrified female voice, soft and flustered, exclaimed from somewhere behind Tony. "Oh, I am so sorry! The most dreadful accident! I cannot apologize enough."

"But it . . . it wasn't!" Tony gasped, still convulsed in hilarity. "I . . . I did it on purpose, and damme, I told you it would work wonders!" Another paroxysm of laughter left him nearly helpless. "No, no, Kev, don't look so murderous. You . . . you would have stepped in that puddle anyway, even if I hadn't forgotten to take the trip line down!"

Cold with fury, Kevin Marlowe gathered what remained

of his dignity and sloshed from the water-filled hole. "I would not, however, have measured my length in it. I collect," he went on in icy tones, "that this is a custom of greeting you have picked up that is common in America?"

"Not for legitimate guests," came the instant retort as the unseen female, who remained just beyond the lantern's light, appeared to rally. "May I inquire what you are doing out here in my stable at this time of night? It is more usual to apply for admittance at the front door!"

"Permit me to inform you, madam, that I did so." He attempted to wring some of the water from his dripping coattails, then gave up in disgust. "I was told by a decidedly forbidding housekeeper that I would find my brother in the stable. As she did not see fit to admit me, I not unnaturally walked out here."

As he moved out of the lantern's bright glare, the figures before him became partially visible in the moonlight. He located his brother, and his words became even more frigid, fairly dripping like icicles. "Am I to believe, Anthony, that you had a valid and sane reason for constructing this . . . this pitfall?"

"It . . . it's not a pitfall!" Tony denied, choking on a fresh wave of unnecessary mirth. "More like a waterfall, Kev. And it wasn't meant for you. Truly, there is a reason for all this, and if you'll just lay those ruffled feathers, I'll explain."

"Tony!" A second female came running up to the group. "Tony, what has happened? Have you caught our villain?"

"No, I'm afraid not. This is more my personal nemesis." His tone still held a reprehensible chuckle.

"Your what?" The girl stared at Kevin's dripping figure, blinking slightly against the bright light of the lantern.

"May I make known to both of you, my brother, Mr. Kevin Marlowe. Mrs. Deane, owner of this farm, and her sister, Miss Isabella Hanley."

Kevin grunted an acknowledgment. "Mrs. Deane and I have met."

The older of the females said, "How do you do," in a voice as cold as his own, and he turned back to Tony.

"Well? I am waiting."

"Really, Kev, you may not know it, but you got off quite

lightly! You might have been coated with molasses and feathers!''

"Anthony, let me tell you—'' he began, and there was real menace in his tone.

"Ben." Mrs. Deane broke across his words, addressing the man with the gun who had been standing by silently during the previous exchange. "Please have Jim and Henry remove all those ridiculous traps at once." Her voice quivered with barely suppressed anger. "Mr. Marlowe, if you will step inside, I will see what can be done to repair the damage to your clothing.''

"Thank you, but no." He shook away a muddy rivulet running down his hand from his soggy coat sleeve. "I have enjoyed quite enough of your hospitality for one night. Anthony, I understand from the Binghams that you rode out here on one of their horses. Kindly recover the animal at once and meet me in front by my carriage." He gave the curtest of bows to the ladies and turned on his heel, the dignity of his retreat somewhat ruined by the squelching of his soggy boots.

Mrs. Deane, after a brief struggle with herself, followed him. "At least allow me to bring you a towel.''

"It is not in the least necessary." He yanked open the entrance gate, and became aware that she had frozen, stock still. Now what ailed the woman?

"Good God," she whispered. "What is that?''

Outlined in the moonlight stood the strangest carriage Charly had ever beheld. The shell-like seat hung suspended in midair, a good ten feet from the ground, slung atop a series of gracefully curved irons. The front wheels were five feet in height, while the back pair rose at least eight. A four-in-hand team stamped nervously, held at the leaders' heads by a boy.

She drew nearer, eyeing it in wonder. "It looks like something out of a fairy tale!''

"It is a crane-necked phaeton, madam." Disdain still colored his voice, but in spite of himself, he was somewhat mollified by her appreciation of his elegant equipage.

"You drive this regularly?" She regarded it critically. "It appears dangerously unstable!''

"It is." He dismissed the danger with an off-hand gesture. At least his exit would be impressive. "I brought it over with me on the ship from England, knowing I would find nothing but the most staid and clumsy vehicles here in the Colonies."

"The States," she corrected.

"The States," he conceded. "Whatever. I find I was quite correct in my assumption. I have not seen its like since I arrived. In London, this type of carriage is all the crack. The Prince of Wales himself drives one just like it."

Nettled by his supercilious tone, Charly shrugged a careless shoulder. "What a foolish reason to risk your neck."

His jaw clenched and his wrath rekindled. Insufferable female! Without another glance at her, he climbed the swaying framework and mounted into the seat. Gathering the reins and collecting his team, he barked a word at the boy, who scrambled onto a shallow step between the back wheels, barely securing his perch before the horses lunged forward.

Tony, coming up just then leading his horse, hurriedly kissed the hand of Bella, who walked at his side.

"I'd best catch him up and explain all this." He leaped up into his saddle. "He's in the devil's own temper," he added cheerfully, and took off at a gallop.

But Charly paid him no heed. She stared after the wildly swaying carriage, watching the effortless control of the furious driver as he disappeared into the darkness. So that was the brother from whom Tony hid! For a fleeting moment, she felt a warm rush of sympathy for the boy. No wonder he ran away to America! So much for her Compleat Horseman. "Bella," she turned to her sister, "did you know Anthony's name was Marlowe? That he was brother to that . . . that man who wouldn't approve my extension?"

"Yes." The answer came in a guilty whisper. "I did not tell you because I feared it would turn you against him."

How right she was! "The man is an odious boor!" It proved her theory, she reflected ruefully. No man could ever live up to a woman's dreams. He might be able to handle any horse, but people seemed to be a different matter.

"He . . . he was rather angry, was he not?" Bella worried

in a very small voice, recalling Charly's attention. They stood by the gate, both distressed by the brothers' uncere-monious departure, though for very different reasons. "I . . . I don't think he liked us," the girl added. "He will not approve of me at all!"

Good! Charlotte thought savagely. Perhaps he would take his precious brother and leave! But her tender heart went out to her stricken sister. Bella would grieve, she knew, if Tony was turned away. And her sister's pain would be much deeper than the disillusionment and emptiness she herself was now experiencing. The Beautiful Tony had been real to Bella, while Charly's Compleat Horseman had been only a dream. And surely, a quick, knife-cut parting would in the long run prove kinder than if Bella was forced to live out a lifetime of regret with a ne'er-do-well for a husband.

Kevin Marlowe, meanwhile, drove back to town at a rate calculated to unship the young tiger clinging frantically to the steps at the rear of his phaeton. Luckily, that worthy had ridden with him enough times before to have learned to wrap his arms and legs about one of the curving iron cranes that held up the bouncing seat and hang on with every ounce of strength he possessed. Only thus would he arrive at the livery stable at the same time as the carriage.

Kevin, about to swing from his high perch, caught sight of the lad's white face. Remorse overcame him. "Lord, Jem lad!" he exclaimed. "I was beyond thinking!"

A groom came forward for the horses and Kevin leaped to the ground. "If ever I do that again, for God's sake, give me a shout!" He favored the boy with a penitent grin. "I'm that sorry, lad!" Steadying the boy, he took some coins from his pocket and pressed them into Jem's hand. "Here, get yourself a pint of ale and a good hot meal." He watched the boy run off stiffly toward an inn across the alley, then started on foot for his hotel. Damn Tony, and damn that female for putting him into such a vile mood!

After he had walked several blocks in wet boots, his temper, which had begun to cool, heated up once more quite nicely. By the time he reached the corner of Wall and Water streets, he found he was looking forward with grim enjoyment to the pleasurable occupation of subjecting Anthony to the most thorough rake-down the boy had ever received in all his young life. And if this was not enough, when he swept through the elaborate portals of the Tontine Coffee House, he experienced the added annoyance of his muddied appearance being the object of shocked stares and considerable comment from a number of well-dressed patrons. One more score against his hapless brother.

He paused at the desk only long enough to request that his man be sent up to his rooms upon the instant, then headed up the stairs. He would comb Tony's hair with a joint-stool, and enjoy every moment of it. Confounded irresponsible young rattle-pate!

Tony had caused him no little trouble of late. He had been forced to chase his brother all the way to America, tracking him by fair means and foul from Boston to New York, only to discover that these Binghams had harbored the boy and let him become infatuated with some American nobody. A proud man, Kevin was not about to tolerate any such connection. He would break up this wretched little affair, he swore. Anthony was not bred to marry a Colonial fortune hunter! He nearly ripped his mud-stained coat as he jerked it off.

Finch, his indispensable man, came in, and life jolted back to a more even keel. With his boots removed, his wet breeches replaced with a dry pair and a brocaded satin dressing gown smoothed across his broad shoulders over a clean linen shirt, he began to feel a measure better. The funny side of his unexpected encounter with the puddle began to emerge, and for a brief instant he teetered on the verge of relating the incident to Finch. But it would be wasted on the man, he realized with sincere regret. His valet, although having no match as curator of a gentleman's wardrobe, was deplorably lacking in a sense of humor.

Clean and comfortable at last, Kevin dismissed the man, selected a poisonous cheroot from the box on his table, and settled back in an armchair to blow a cloud as he awaited Anthony's inevitable arrival. Knowing his brother, his explanation of the night's events—not to mention those of the past few months—should prove highly diverting.

In crediting his brother with a lively imagination, Kevin acted on knowledge of old. It had been his fate over the years to rescue his scrape-grace sibling from any number of peculiar circumstances in which the boy's sportive and inventive genius had entangled him. This one would be no different. He could only be surprised that Anthony had eluded him for so long.

For once, the brothers were in complete agreement. The half-hour's ride back into town left Tony plenty of time to think. His surprise, he realized, lay not in Kevin's sudden arrival at Deane Farm, but in the fact that his capable brother had not put in an appearance much earlier. He had expected to be caught long before now! In fact, had Tony not paused to indulge in an elegant bit of dalliance with the loveliest girl he had ever encountered, he would have been on his way again days ago, though not to Philadelphia with George Bingham. From that worthy, he had gained a gloomy view of America's new capital. The Quakers, George said, frowned on all fashionable dress and amusements of every kind. Not at all the place for Tony Marlowe.

Well, he reflected, it was his own fault for indulging his flirtatious nature. Kevin had him fairly caught, and he'd best face the music. He might, of course, concoct some marvelous tale for Kev's edification, but his brother had an uncanny and unsettling ability to see through every subterfuge. No, a highly colored version of the truth would be more likely to appeal to Kev's strong sense of the ridiculous.

He slowed to a steady trot, giving himself more time to plan. It would do no harm to let Kev cool off a bit, but not for too long. Patience was not his middle name. He was in for a rare dressing down, no two ways about it. He had best prepare himself by putting on his most virtuous and candid expression. That, he knew of old, was the only way to get around old Kev. Leaving the horse at the Binghams' and ascertaining from them the name of his brother's hotel, he walked over, practicing as he went how to look humble and innocent.

His luck was in. His delaying had allowed just enough time for Kevin to discover an excellent brandy hidden away in the hotel cellar. Under the influence of several glasses, he was quite willing to listen to Tony's version of the evening's events.

"But with none of your fancy elaborations," he told his brother strictly. "Let us have the whole tale without roundaboutation."

Tony was a past master at relating comic incidents. In his element, he soon put Kevin in possession of the facts as far as he knew them, only letting himself go a bit as he described the beautiful traps they had set to catch the prowler.

Kevin leaned back in his chair, sipping his brandy and regarding his young brother thoughtfully. An expert at reading between the lines—and jumping to conclusions—he noted that Miss Hanley's name had been deleted rather pointedly from Anthony's story. His suspicions were confirmed. Anthony's flirtation—an inevitable happening wherever the boy went—had gone deeper this time than perhaps his silly gudgeon of a brother intended or even realized. Clever Miss Hanley.

The sisters were in financial difficulties, he knew, and now with the death of the stallion, their situation must be critical. Already, he had suspected Miss Isabella Hanley of being a fortune hunter. Tony said Mrs. Deane seemed to disapprove of him. If this was to be believed, it could only be that she hoped to force a price from him to save Tony from their clutches. Well, he'd soon see about that. Dismissing his brother with only a few well-chosen words, he prepared for bed—and battle.

The next morning, leaving Tony with orders to remain in the city, Kevin drove out to Deane Farm with the intention of having a quiet confrontation with Mrs. Deane. The sooner he learned with what sort of female he had to deal, the sooner he would be able to extricate his brother and go home. He had no desire to remain in America a moment longer than necessary.

The ride, in the crisp morning breeze, did much to mellow his mood. He was even able to admire the view afforded of the farm as he crested the last, low hill. It was a beautiful place, he had to admit, with a respectable house, well laid out barns, and extensive pastureland.

He drew his team up before the gates and jumped down, handing his reins to his tiger. No one was in sight. He strode up to the door and knocked, only to find himself once more before the acid-faced housekeeper.

"Is Mrs. Deane at home?" he asked with a fixed smile on his face. The woman looked him over scathingly and gave him to understand that to see "Charlie" he would have to go out to the barn.

A trifle mystified, he headed out around the house, wondering who this Charlie was and why he must see him first. At the gate to the paddock area, he strode past a huge puddle and noted the length of looped-back rope that had proved his downfall the night before. Not very original, perhaps, but quite effective. He had to give Anthony credit for that. At least the way now seemed safe.

He saw no one at the first two barns but, as he approached the third, he heard someone shouting. Quickening his pace, he looked in. A gray mare lay on her side in the straw. Crouched by her hind quarters, a slight youth, wearing a worn leather jerkin and ancient buckskin breeches far too big for him, held the head of a newborn foal in his lap.

A braid of taffy-colored hair swung as he turned. "Thank God someone has come!"

Marlowe stared, aghast. It was a female—it was Mrs. Deane! A dirty-faced, slovenly American savage! What on earth could Tony be thinking of, flirting with one of her family!

"You fool!" she shouted at him. "Don't just stand there! Get Ben for me, hurry! He's in the back pasture repairing the fence with the boys and they cannot hear me!"

A retort had formed on his lips, when it suddenly dawned on him that she was in real difficulty. From the frantic expression on her terrified face, he realized there was something seriously amiss. Without thinking, he peeled off his coat and ran into the box. "What's happened?"

"It's not breathing!"

He threw down his coat. "Dammit, put that head down!" At least she had stripped away the caul. Roughly shoving

her aside, he caught up the foal by its hind legs and with
brute strength, raised it high, letting the head dangle. Mrs.
Deane shrieked and grabbed at the baby.

"Quickest way," he snapped. "No time to waste. We
have to drain the fluid from its throat, and shaking down the
internal organs onto the heart and lungs may stimulate them
to function."

He lowered the foal back down on the straw. "Now get
something . . . a towel . . . anything at hand and rub!" Already, he was massaging the colt's neck and chest, trying to
force it to take a breath. Mrs. Deane scrubbed at the body
with handfuls of straw.

"Oh, it's not working!" she gasped.

Marlowe could see that it was not. Holding his fingers
over one of the foal's nostrils, he blew into the other, waited
a few seconds, and blew again.

"The ribs," he ordered. "Press up and down. Gently!"
he added as she obeyed too eagerly. He breathed again into
the foal, trying to fill its little lungs.

Suddenly he stopped and sat back. She stared at him, the
blood drained from her face.

"It . . . it's dead?"

"Not this time." He grinned, and mingled triumph and
relief transformed his harsh expression.

To Charly, the man sitting in the straw beside the breathing foal seemed almost godlike. She dashed away tears that
formed unbidden. "How can I thank you?"

Kevin rose, sweeping straw from his breeches. "Thank
me? Why, by telling me the way to the nearest pump. I fear
I am a bit soiled. No, don't leave that foal. It may be an
hour or more before it gains the strength to stand. Keep
rubbing it down. Here." He took off his neckcloth, a yard or
more of foot-wide linen. "Use this. It's ruined anyway."

Meekly Charly accepted it. "There's a pump and trough
outside."

The mare had pulled her forelegs beneath her and now
lunged to her feet. She bent her head and began licking her
new foal, making soft, whickering noises of encouragement
deep in her throat. Charly and Zephyr worked together on
the colt. As Marlowe returned, shaking water from his

hands, the foal raised its head. He nodded, satisfied. "It will live."

Charly's eyes met his, her heart too full for words, and for a moment their gaze held, both lost in the wonder and joy of a new life saved. It was he who broke the spell, looking a bit startled. He turned away, bending to inspect the afterbirth, making sure it was complete.

Charly stared at Kevin Marlowe's broad back in its soiled linen shirt, and a flood of gratitude washed through her. Her Compleat Horseman. He had certainly proved himself this day, using that magic touch, his innate ability, to save her beloved Zephyr's foal. Stammering, she started again to thank him, then couldn't stop talking. She was babbling, she knew, in the release of her terror, telling him just how much this colt meant to her.

"He will be the salvation of Deane Farm, I know it! It was my husband's dream, this bloodline, and when I lost Summer Storm it seemed to be the end. This foal will eventually take his place as my stud, and I'll breed the perfect cross for racing."

They watched Zephyr nosing the new baby. "He's half Arabian from Zephyr, his dam," Charly continued, still talking, not knowing how to stop. "And half thoroughbred from his sire. Summer Storm was a beauty." Her voice caught, and she swallowed. "He had the size, the strength, to combine with the speed of my mares . . ."

"Hard to tell about this one yet, but he looks a bit light," Kevin stated.

"He's to race on the flat, not be a jumper." She smiled at her new colt through eyes half blinded by misty tears. Emotion flooded through her, and she let her breath out in a long sigh. It seemed as though, at last, her troubles were on the way to being over.

Kevin stroked Zephyr's neck, and the mare turned to poke her nose at his shoulder. She accepted him, a stranger, allowing him near her and her new foal. The Compleat Horseman, of course. A growing warmth filled Charly. She had recognized it in the man the first time she saw him riding that bone-jarring hack before Mr. Van Bleek's house.

And she knew it again now overwhelmingly, watching him with her beloved mare.

For the first time, she really looked at the man. He rolled his sleeves down over muscular arms, then bent to retrieve his coat from where he'd thrown it down on the straw. His every movement spoke of leashed power, of carefully controlled muscle. He must be thirty-five, at least, she decided, admiring the effect of those becoming wings of gray at each temple.

As he worked his way into his smooth-fitting coat, he turned and smiled with devastating effect. Suddenly, startlingly, his resemblance to Tony leaped out at her. He was not as tall as his brother, but broader, and his features were rough-hewn instead of classically beautiful, but the family resemblance was strong. With his size, his weight, and heavier features, she thought he looked a Mars to Tony's Apollo, and then was annoyed with herself for thinking anything so fanciful.

She blinked back the rosy aura that seemed to surround him and forced herself to look with the eyes of reality. And she gasped. His fine linen shirt was not just muddied, it was ruined! And his pale fawnskin breeches were hopelessly stained and his coat spattered with muck.

"Oh, dear," she cried. "Your clothes! Oh, they are quite spoiled."

He looked down at himself in surprise. His breeches were beyond even Finch's ability to save, and his boots would never be the same. He laughed, a short, mirthless bark. "Damme, I forgot everything but saving that foal!"

"And I can't tell you how grateful I am!" Tears sprang to Charly's eyes. "Indeed, I do not think I have yet thanked you enough for all you did. And I do, most sincerely. I do not know what I would have done had you not come along."

He looked down at her quizzically. "No, you would have fared ill, would you not? Surely this example must prove to you the foolishness of being a female in this business. You cannot continue here alone."

Her quick temper flared, gratitude forgotten. "I can and I will! In spite of you, Mr. Marlowe."

He shrugged. "I fail to see where it would spite me."

Charly stared at him. Could he not know Van Bleek had given her the extension over his objections? At that moment the colt managed to gain its feet, taking a few unsteady steps, falling down, and scrambling awkwardly back up. Marlowe looked it over more critically.

"At any rate, that's not going to be the horse you need," he pronounced at last, shaking his head. "Far too light boned."

Charly gasped at this slight to the darling of her hopes. "He is the image of Summer Storm!"

He shook his head again. "You need a heavier stud. You have a good mare here, and she may have the speed you want, but she's passed on her Arabian delicacy and fine bones. You need to add more strength and brawn. Now in Ireland, I have a horse—"

"Thank you," she snapped. "I have heard all about your Excalibur from your brother. I want America to have light flat racers, not those heavy steeplechasers that you have in Ireland. I'm breeding for speed."

"No, now, you're going about it all wrong." He leaned his shoulders against the barn wall and proceeded to lecture. "A good racehorse must have more than speed. He'll need solid hindquarters to be able to make that starting lunge. Once out first, ahead of the pack, he merely needs to run as fast as the others to hold that lead. What you require, horse lady, is more muscle in your stock."

Charly caught back an angry retort. He criticized the very foundation of what she was trying to do! And a niggling fear that he just might be right made his comments doubly unwelcome. Managing to remember that at the moment she stood deeply in his debt and that it behooved her to be polite, she changed the touchy subject to one she was sure he'd appreciate.

"Tell me about your horse. How did you come to name him Excalibur?"

It did the trick. He came off his lecture platform and relaxed. "It seemed natural. He's silver gray, you see, and the first time I laid eyes on him, he was coming up out of a lake."

"He swims?"

Marlowe grinned, once more resembling the charming Tony, and sent her wayward heart fluttering. "Of course. Many horses do when they have the opportunity."

"Zephyr plays in the trough." Unwilling to surrender, she looked away, transferring her gaze to the mare. Her expression softened, and she laughed. "Perhaps we should dig her a lake."

"She would probably enjoy it," he agreed. "A good deal more than I did." He laughed with her, and an odd happiness filled her. "My horses like to swim. Fortunately, my lake already existed." A reminiscent light kindled in his eyes and that irrepressible grin tugged at the corners of his mouth. "I will never forget one day. I'd been schooling Excalibur over fences. When we came to the lake, I couldn't resist the temptation to go for a swim. Neither could he. Followed me right in and soaked a good saddle!"

He chuckled softly, and she joined in the rich, infectious sound, welcoming an unfamiliar understanding with a kindred soul. They were two true horse lovers talking about their favorite subject, and she felt something deeper, more complex than mere friendship begin to form between them. Forgetting for the moment their differing opinions on her race stock, she mentioned an upcoming event at Hempstead Plains on the Long Island barrens, where the first formal horse races had been held in 1660.

"I plan to have a horse entered," she said proudly. "One of Storm's first foals. Summer Wind. He's a sure winner."

Marlowe raised skeptical eyebrows. "And do you fancy him a successor to the great Eclipse?" he asked. A teasing note lurked in his voice.

"Perhaps not Wind," she admitted with reluctance. "And you need not look so surprised. Your reference does not confound me. Even in America, we have heard of that legendary English racehorse. Did you know, there were racers here who went into mourning for Eclipse when he died in '89? But one of my horses will one day equal his record!"

Kevin threw his head back and laughed outright, but with a gruding admiration. "That is hardly a usual ambition for a female! At least you have spirit and determination. You are going to need plenty of both in this field. I wish you luck, horse lady, may you become another James De Lancy.''

Charly smiled sweetly, hiding her irritation at yet another male's insufferable opinion that horse breeding was no line of work for a woman. ''Oh, I could hardly be that. He was known as the Father of the American Turf, you know. It takes a man to be a father, and I am naught but a mere female, remember?''

''When you wear those breeches, it is hard to do so.''

Charly flushed. ''Sir, I have much work to do that cannot be done in skirts. If you will excuse me, I must get back to it.''

He caught her arm as she prepared to stalk angrily away. ''Nay, now. Let's not come to cuffs. I was funning, only. My apologies. I daresay your horse will make a good showing.'' This last was said in the condescending manner of one offering an olive branch.

She whirled on him. ''Good showing, indeed! You will see! Wind will win easily. In fact,'' she informed him loftily, ''your brother Tony is begging to ride him in the race meet for me!''

He frowned. ''That brings me to the reason I drove out here this morning.'' He ran a hand through his already disordered dark locks. ''This affair with your sister will not do. I must tell you that I intend to put an end to it.''

Charly's eyes opened wide in relieved surprise. She began to stammer her complete agreement with this plan, but he waved a peremptory hand, silencing her.

''Hear me out, if you please. I have arranged an excellent alliance for Tony in England, one that will raise our family to the eminence it once knew. He is already betrothed.''

Charly blinked, shocked. So Tony's intentions toward her sister were not honorable! There had always been that fear, but she had tried to ignore it, not wanting to believe it possible. No wonder learning of their financial problems had not put him off, she thought savagely. If anything, he must feel it put him in a better bargaining position for Bella's favors. And when he was through with her, he would return home to this advantageous match his brother had arranged!

"So he is to marry for money!" She wrinkled her nose in distaste, repelled by such mercenary plans. "He ... you both are nothing more than a pair of gazetted fortune hunters!" Now she would be happier than ever, she told herself, to see the last of Tony Marlowe—and his odious brother Kevin as well!

Marlowe straightened up to his full height and looked down his very aristocratic nose, his eyebrows raised at this accusation of vulgarity. "Certainly not! My own fortune is more than sufficient. But it is one I earned in India, after my father wasted our estate."

She must have appeared every bit as perplexed as she felt, for he explained curtly, as though deigning to enlighten American ignorance. "I am a nabob. My money is derived from trade. I may be wealthy, but socially I am an outcast from the London *ton*. I now intend to see our family restored to respectability through Anthony's marriage to a lady of birth and breeding. For the last year, my every effort has been devoted to arranging this marriage for him to a titled lady, only to have the young fool run off."

"That must have upset the lady," she remarked acidly, while secretly applauding Tony's gumption in avoiding such a distasteful match.

Kevin ignored her comment. "I explained to her father that Anthony had gone on a pleasure jaunt, wishing to see something of the world before he settles down. I intend him to return to England at once."

"I see." Charlotte's tone was derisive. "You hope to scale the social ladder on your brother's shoulders."

He shrugged. "It must be Tony. I have not the looks for such a marriage."

"Nor the manners," she shot back. "Speaking of breeding! We in America do not stoop so low!" She squared off, ready for the inevitable quarrel.

He merely shrugged, refusing to see anything wrong with his ambition. "My money and Tony's handsome face for the noble lady's social standing. It seems to me—and to her—a fair exchange."

"Fair!"

"At any rate, you may tell your sister to stop casting out

lures for Tony, for she will never succeed. Tony has no money, remember . . . it is mine. Tony's future is arranged." In his annoyance at Anthony, he forgot momentarily to whom he was speaking. "I'll not have him taken in by a horde of country bumpkins aping the high society of their betters in England. This tawdry little affair with your sister is at an end!"

Without thinking, Charly grabbed the bucket from which Zephyr had been drinking and threw the water over him, abruptly ending the interview.

CHAPTER
Seven

*S*omewhat surprised to find that he was not angry, Kevin Marlowe climbed up into the high, swaying seat of his phaeton and signaled his tiger to "let them go." His coat front, shirt, and breeches were soaked, and water dripped onto the leather seat. Was he always to leave Deane Farm in this condition?

He didn't blame that little firebrand. It was all the fault of the too-quick tongue he had never learned to guard. Heaving that bucket of water over him was just what he might have done himself had he been so insulted, although he'd have been more likely to draw his opponent's cork. She could hardly do that, he decided as he drove his team down the lane at an unusually decorous pace. Granted, she had done the next best thing.

She had spirit, that yellow-haired horse lady. He liked spirit in a filly and he liked it in a woman. It would be interesting to see if he could tame her. Too bad she was an American savage, or he would be tempted to try. Wearing men's buckskins, yet! And a face so dirty it was next to impossible to make out her features! A pity—he rather liked her, but she was devilish hard on his clothes. This was the second coat she'd ruined. A regular little shrew! Would she, he wondered, if he had the time, ever play Kate to his Petrucchio?

Could he make the time . . . ?

* * *

His "Kate," meanwhile, stalked back to the house, fuming. So they were a horde of country bumpkins, were they? Tawdry little affair indeed! How dare a confessed social climber like Mr. Kevin Marlowe say such things to her, a Hanley of New York City!

How could he be so exactly what she wanted in a man, everything she had longed for all her life, and yet be so . . . so . . . !

She slammed the door and ran upstairs, where she threw herself, dirty clothes and all, onto her bed and pounded both fists into the pillow. Oh, how right she had been about him the night before. He might be a marvel when it came to horses, but in all other respects, her Compleat Horseman had feet of clay. She smiled, grimly, appreciating her choice of phrase. More like feet of muck and mud! Not for ages had she enjoyed anything as much as the sight of him spluttering from the contents of that bucket!

And little though he knew it, he had also solved one of her problems. When Bella learned of Tony's engagement, she would be only too quick to denounce him for the cad he was. It would hurt at first, but she would get over it. And the Beautiful Tony was not the only fish in the sea of New York society. A girl as lovely as Bella would always be sought after. She would tell her at once. She paused, but then . . .

It was not the vision of a tearful Bella that gave her pause. It was the recollection of her sister's romantic nature. Already aware of Charly's disapproval of her idolized Tony, would she not be suspicious of this tale of a former betrothal? If the girl confronted young Mr. Marlowe, would he confirm its truth? Or would he take the opportunity to set the sisters against each other, thus securing for himself a very innocent and angry prize? Bella already half fancied herself a Juliet; who knew to what lengths she would go to prove her love?

Slowly Charly got up again and walked back downstairs and out to the paddock, where she could think this out. She dared not take the chance. She could, of course, tell Bella of the opposition of Tony's brother. But secretly, she feared that would not weigh with the girl. It would cast Tony in the role of a persecuted Romeo, and truly bring on the situation

she feared. Her best course, she decided with regret, would
be to say nothing.

"Charly!" Bella, leaning out of a window on the second
story, waved frantically to her. "Where have you been? It is
time and more that we were leaving for New York! Surely
you have not forgotten the Ridgeways' rout tonight!"

"Zephyr has foaled!" she shouted back. "We have our
colt!"

Bella squealed, and the lovely golden head disappeared
from the window. Charly waited, and in moments her sister
came full fling out the back door.

"Why did you not call me?" the girl demanded as she
ran down the path to the mare's barn.

"I tried." Briefly—and downplaying the role of Kevin
Marlowe—she told Bella about the morning's work. The
sight of mare and foal, both doing fine, sent Bella into
transports. Ben had already refilled the water bucket, Charly
noted without the least remorse.

As they returned to the house, Bella, still overcome with
delight, practically skipped along the path, chattering about the
colt's undoubtedly brilliant future. In her excitement, she never
questioned the presence of Tony's brother at the foaling. With
this birth, she firmly seemed to believe all of their problems
were immediately as good as solved. The mortgage now could
be repaid and all would continue as normal at Deane Farm.

If only it could be that easy, Charly reflected when,
bathed and gowned, she at last climbed into the seat of the
light chaise. Bella scrambled up beside her, and they set off
for the drive back to Aunt Augusta's house. How relieved
that lady would be to see them—Bella giggled—and how
she would laugh to learn that Charly had indeed been called
upon to hold the mare's "hoof" for the foaling!

With the safe arrival of the foal, and the farm left in
Ben's capable hands, Charly once again turned her thoughts
to Bella and the social whirl of the Season. In this, she was
ably supported by Augusta Hanley. No sooner did that lady
learn that all went well at the farm than she began to review
the plans for Bella's birthday ball.

"Bella's presentation ball shall be as nothing compared

with this!'' She handed Charly a long list of names. ''Only see all to whom I have sent invitations.''

Charly glanced at the sheet and a name caught her eye. ''Simone Galbraith? Has she not a somewhat questionable reputation?''

Augusta sniffed. ''She is not yet so daring as to have been excluded from society. Her husband's wealth guarantees her entry. If Ephraim Galbraith weren't senile, he'd keep a better guard on the hussy. He was a fool to marry a woman half his age, and French at that. I felt obliged to include her. After all, one meets her everywhere.''

''Still . . .'' Charly shrugged and handed back the list. ''Well, you know best.''

''And we can invite Tony Marlowe, can we not?'' Bella begged before Charly could stop her.

Aunt Augusta, who had been told of his deception, hesitated, a slight frown creasing her brow. She glanced at Charlotte, over Bella's head.

''Of course we shall, dearest.'' Charly threw her aunt a speaking look, which that lady had no trouble interpreting. Opposition must not take an open form. After all, a great deal could happen in a day or so. Mr. Kevin Marlowe looked like a man who was accustomed to getting his own way, and he meant to end the affair. On this one subject only, were he and Charly in accord.

The rout did much to restore Charly's temper, for neither Kevin Marlowe nor his brother Tony were present. Nor was Jonathan Treadwell. For Charly, it seemed the evening would be calm and peaceful.

That mood lasted for perhaps five minutes. As she strolled across the drawing room, a contemporary of her aunt's gestured hopefully to her. Having no wish to slight so kindly a creature as Miss Anabel Brougham, she hurried over.

''So delightful to see you in colors once more, my dear,'' Miss Brougham gushed, her bright, eager eyes on Charly's face. ''And sweet Isabella looks a dream.'' She looked pointedly about the room. ''But such a shame that young Mr. Marlowe is not here.''

''Is it?'' Charly asked, a bit of frost in her voice.

"Oh, you are not saying anything yet, my dear, and I am sure I do not blame you. Just known in the family, then? Such a delightful couple as they make! So very beautiful to look at. How happy you and dear Augusta must be." This last was accompanied by a sly wink.

Charly managed a slight smile. "Why, I believe you make too much of it," she replied, carefully keeping her tone light. "There has been no talk of such a thing. They are but children, after all. I pray you will not repeat such a ridiculous thought to anyone. It would quite embarrass them, you must know, and put a strain on their friendship."

Miss Brougham blinked, her expression comical in its dismay. "No, oh, no, of course not, my dear Charlotte. I only thought . . . that is . . . well, they do make such a lovely couple, dancing together. When one grows old, one hopes to see romance." The elderly lady sighed with obvious disappointment.

Charly forced a light laugh and strolled on. A pretty feeble attempt to quell gossip, she reflected, but what could she say? That there was no thought of marriage because the Beautiful Tony merely indulged himself in a last fling at the expense of the innocent Bella before returning to England and an arranged advantageous marriage? That Bella, and the whole Hanley family, were not good enough for the precious Marlowes?

Charlotte found no further pleasure in the party. Retiring among the chaperons, she kept a close eye on her lively sister. The girl behaved exactly as she ought, never standing up more than twice with any gentleman, showing no preference for one over another and enjoying the company of all. Still, it was with relief that Charly finally called for their carriage and took her sister home.

The absence of Tony Marlowe from the Ridgeways' rout proved to be an isolated occurrence. His circle of acquaintances had grown, and despite Charly's hopes, his departure for England did not appear imminent. They met him everywhere they went, and his standing up with Bella became a very familiar if unwelcome sight. Why had his odious brother not taken Tony away?

Try as she might, Charly by herself could hit upon no

scheme to break up this affair without alienating Bella—or worse, driving her straight into Tony's eager arms. She could only hope that he would either tire of the game, which seemed unlikely, or try to force her sister's hand. He did not seem one to rush his fences, though.

Her first warning of real danger came at a dinner party three days later. Miss Anabel Brougham, Aunt Augusta's talkative friend, drew her firmly aside, her gentle eyes holding an unusual martial light.

"You know I am not one to carry tales, my dear," she remarked mendaciously, filling Charlotte with a sense of deep foreboding. "But this time I saw them myself, and knew I must drop just a word of warning in your ear. Not a vestige of a chaperon!" She shook her head, clicking her tongue in disapproval.

"What did you see?" Charlotte asked after a moment's hesitation. If the gossip was spreading, she had best know the truth.

"Why, Isabella and Mr. Marlowe, walking alone together in City Hall Park, and no Miss Nidbury in sight!"

"If Niddy could not accompany her, then I can only be glad she found Mr. Marlowe to see that she came to no harm," Charlotte shot back. A feeble projectile, she knew, but she could not allow this to go unanswered.

Nor was the subsequent interview with her sister any more satisfactory. "I could hardly repulse him!" Bella declared. "I was walking with Joanna Bedford, only she wanted to join several friends and I wished to return home. I was quite at a loss until I saw Tony. It was most kind in him to offer to escort me, and I think you should thank him rather than criticize!" The bright blue eyes met Charly's in challenge.

"I have to tell you it caused some very unpleasant gossip," Charly informed her sister sternly.

Bella's cheeks paled, then brightened with warm color. "How . . . how unkind! As if there was anything wrong! Tony is a perfect gentleman. I am sure I am safer with him than with anyone!"

Prudently, Charly let the subject drop. Bella had been warned, and a more pointed order would only set her flying to the defense of her Beautiful Tony. From here, she must guide her sister with care. A child not yet eighteen hadn't the experience to know when—or even how—to draw the line.

And where, Charly fumed, was Kevin Marlowe? If it was indeed his intention to break up this "tawdry little affair," he certainly seemed in no hurry. She had not seen him since that morning four days ago when she had dumped Zephyr's bucket of water over his head. The memory brought her a certain satisfaction. But still the question bothered her. Where was he and what was he doing?

At a venetian breakfast the next morning, she put the question to Tony himself.

"Oh, he's gone back to Boston on business," he informed her carelessly.

The news came as a severe blow. Had he come to the same conclusion as she, that Tony merely trifled with Bella? If so, Kevin would be quite willing to allow the flirtation to run its course. It would make no difference to his plans for Tony's marriage. Nor would he spare a single thought for the damage to Bella's trusting heart—or her reputation. He was an odious man! The opprobrium that so frequently sprang to her mind truly applied!

Charly wondered what would happen if Tony should persuade Bella to return with him to England. Perhaps—a frightening thought—on the pretext of marrying her there, and then convincing the gullible girl to remain as his mistress while he married as his brother ordered, to gain the money to support her on the side. No! She gave herself a vigorous mental shake. That was utter nonsense! Bella would never consent to such an arrangement.

The last few days had passed in a busy blur of catching up on relatives, forgotten connections, and old friends from before her marriage to Abner Deane and her subsequent retirement to the country. Now Charly escaped for a few precious hours to visit her mare. All progressed well, to her relief. No further mysterious or deadly incidents had occurred, and her fears for Deane Farm began to recede. She even convinced herself that Ben had been mistaken about

Summer Storm. No one would have shot her horse deliberately. The idea, as she had thought at the time, was ludicrous. The intruder she had surprised in the barn that night must have been nothing more than a stray prowler. Now if only Wind lived up to his promise!

Bella continued blissfully happy, still glorying in the round of routs, drums, and balls. But mostly, Charly feared, it was the continuing attentions of Tony Marlowe that brought the soft flush to Bella's cheeks and the sparkling glow to her lovely blue eyes.

"I must be the envy of every other girl," Bella breathed to her sister one evening after Tony returned her to Charlotte's side.

"I am certain you are." There was no doubt of that. Charly attempted to keep her bitterness from creeping into her voice. The Beautiful Tony attracted worshippers everywhere he went. Why on earth could he not turn to any one of the other love-struck maidens who flirted with him in the most outrageous manner? Unfortunately, they only had the opportunity whenever he was forced by the dictates of convention to stand up with someone besides Bella, his acknowledged favorite. At least, as Charly was somewhat relieved to discover, he realized the necessity to preserve Bella from gossip by soliciting her hand for only the acceptable two dances. But this good was mitigated by the fact that his eyes followed her around the floor throughout the evening.

To Charly's mixed dismay and relief, Tony Marlowe still had not offered for Bella's hand. He pursued her in the most gallant manner, spared no effort to engage her affections, but never, not by even the most casual reference, did he indicate that he wanted a more permanent connection with the girl.

This fact seemed at last to have dawned on Bella. Charly, anxiously watching her sister, noted with unease the nervous flicking of the girl's fan as she withdrew with the Beautiful Tony to a window embrasure during an interlude between dances. When the two separated, it was at Bella's instigation, and she went at once to join a small group who stood talking near a refreshment table. Very casually, she came up beside Mr. Richard Cranford. That gentleman greeted her warmly; Bella responded in kind; and when the group moved apart, Bella walked off on Mr. Cranford's arm.

Was she trying to make Tony Marlowe jealous? Now, where had the little minx learned that trick? Charly glanced at Tony, and found him in conversation with a ravishing brunette. He appeared to derive no pleasure in her company; his eyes strayed often to Bella, and his manner could only be described as annoyed.

So her little sister sought to bring her elusive suitor up to scratch, did she? Charly's heart sank. More like, she would drive him into some ill-judged action, such as coaxing her to fly with him, without benefit of clergy—a fact he would be sure not to mention until it was too late.

Nor did she like Bella's leading on Mr. Cranford. Aside from his being the nephew of General Parks, Charly quite liked the man and knew him to be more than mildly partial to her lively sister. More than once, she had suspected him of trying to fix his interest with the girl, but Bella's infatuation with Tony led her to turn a deaf ear to his opening gambits. Encouragement such as he now received might cause him to indulge unwarranted hopes.

Disturbed, Charly turned away, only to find herself face-to-face with Jonathan Treadwell. This was all she needed! She smiled and tried to sidestep him. It was not to work.

He caught her hand, beaming down at her in a fatuous manner. "You are looking uncommonly beautiful this evening," he murmured.

"Effusive compliments?" She raised an eyebrow in mild surprise. "I thought you preferred plain speaking."

"I prefer to please you." He ventured a gallant response that failed to move her.

She sighed. Nothing seemed to discourage him. Tilting her head sideways, she regarded him through narrowed eyes. On the whole, she could not decide whether she was more irritated by his refusal to take no for an answer, or for the condescending way in which he presumed that she had no other choice and that it was merely a matter of time before she was forced to sell up her farm and surrender.

Briefly, she considered casting out a lure toward Richard Cranford herself for the pure joy of confounding Jonathan's detestable smugness.

For once, Augusta Hanley proved an unsatisfactory confidant. When Charly laughingly told her of her idea the following morning, her aunt merely shook her head.

"It would do no good, my dear. Jonathan knows that Richard Cranford has eyes only for Bella." August gave a small, satisfied smile. "Such a perfect connection as that would be, do you not think? Mr. Cranford's manners and address must make him acceptable anywhere."

Charly flounced off, for once out of charity with her favorite relative.

Charly still had not decided how to deal with her unwanted suitor when he came up to her at the Bedfords' ball two days later. He bowed low before her, took her hand firmly in his, and tried very hard to make her meet his eyes.

"The next dance is mine," he informed her.

"Jonathan, you know I do not dance this evening." She tried to pull her hand free. "I am here only as Bella's chaperon."

He retained his hold. "Nonsense. Your sister has not been near you for the past hour and more. And you will hardly be criticized for standing up with me." Over her protests, he pulled her onto the floor to join the set just forming.

Detesting the public scene that would be necessary to escape him, she gave in, silently racking up one more score against him. In her mind, a real gentleman did not place a lady in such a position. As the dance drew to a close, she turned pointedly away, only to have him take her arm with a possessive air and draw her toward the refreshment table.

The next set began almost at once, and she found it impossible to escape from Jonathan as he led her to a chair at the side of the room. Her temper rose, and she longed to dress him down in rare style. A few more minutes of his company and she might forget their surroundings and indulge herself. She turned on him, her eyes glittering, but her opening words were halted by an unexpected interruption.

"Charlotte, my dear." Miss Anabel Brougham stood

before her, her smooth brow puckered in a frown. "May I have a word with you? Pray excuse us, Mr. Treadwell."

"Of course." Charly stood at once, handing her half-full glass to the annoyed Jonathan. "Come, I see an empty bench just over here."

Miss Brougham accompanied her a few steps, then slowed. "No need to sit down. Have you seen Isabella?"

"Not since she was last dancing with..." Charlotte broke off, for there was Bella, going down a country dance again with Tony Marlowe.

"Exactly," said Miss Brougham, in a shocked, hushed voice. "This is the *third* dance, and in a row, mind you, that they have shared! You'd best have a care lest she supplant Mrs. Galbraith as the favorite victim of the scandalmongers."

Charlotte gasped. She could not bear the thought of her innocent young sister's name mentioned in the same breath as that dishonorable matron! How could she have so neglected her duty! Oh, it was all Jonathan Treadwell's fault for monopolizing her and making her so very angry that she had forgotten everything else.

And as for the Beautiful Tony: so much for his sense of propriety! Or more importantly, so much for his having a care to Bella's reputation. Charly nearly groaned aloud. He would soon have Bella socially ruined, and it was obvious he did not care. Was he leading up to something? Had Bella's flirtation with Richard Cranford worked too well on Tony? This time, she would have no choice but to bring her sister to book.

The scene, which Charly delayed until the following morning, proved every bit as unpleasant as she had feared. Bella stared at her, her face turning first white and then a vivid red, and tears starting to her eyes.

"How... how cruel those horrid gossips can be! There was no harm in my dancing with him!"

"No, of course there wasn't," Charly said, trying to maintain calm. "The harm lay in defying convention."

"It is a silly convention! We were having the most delightful conversation; neither of us wished to break it off!"

Charly bit back a sharp retort. It was impossible to carry on a conversation when one was constantly separated by the movements of the dance and Bella knew it. "Conventions are meant to guide conduct. When you are seen to ignore one, you are suspected of ignoring others as well."

Bella shrugged a defiant shoulder. "It makes no matter. The foolish gossip will stop soon enough." A slight, triumphant smile played about her lips.

Charly regarded her sister in growing dismay. "Do you mean he has offered for you? Without first approaching your guardian?"

"Well, no." Bella plucked at a sprigged flower on the narrow skirt of her muslin gown. "But he will offer soon. I am quite certain of it. That is . . ." She broke off, raising eyes brimful of happiness to her sister. "That is why I danced so often with him last night. I . . . I just know he is on the verge."

Charly did not doubt it either, though what, precisely, she believed him to be on the verge *of* was quite another matter. With a strict warning to remember Aunt Augusta's sensibilities, and not to give the old tabbies any more fodder for unkind gossip, she left Bella with, she hoped, ample food for thought.

Only too soon Charly was caught up in a whirl of activity as they prepared for Bella's birthday. Everything must be different, Augusta decreed, from their last ball, which had been held less than a month before. The music, the decorations, especially the refreshments and supper menu, must all be unique, not the same routine they had encountered at every ball this season. Theirs, Augusta informed them loftily, would be an Occasion to be remembered!

This prophecy proved to be correct. When the thirty guests, carefully chosen from the cream of New York Society, sat down to dinner, nothing could rival the elegance of the dining room. Augusta had personally selected the menu, and not a single delicacy had been omitted. Hours had been spent discussing with Miss Nidbury the relative virtues of Gowanus oysters stewed in cream, dressed lobster, semelles of redfish, filets of veal, roasted ducklings, quails with chevreuil sauce, all to be washed down with fine wine, five kinds of champagne, and port for the gentlemen. A string quartet played softly in the far corner, providing delightful background music throughout the meal.

But as far as Bella was concerned, there was a vastly important omission. Anthony Marlowe was not to be among the dinner guests. When she first discovered this, Bella had run to her aunt, demanding that the error be corrected upon the instant. It was her party, after all.

But saner reason prevailed. Did she want the gossips to set up Tony's back? Charly asked diplomatically. For one of her many suitors to be singled out above the others would give rise to the most vulgar speculation. She would be known to have set her cap for him. Nothing could be more distasteful to a gentleman.

That gave Bella pause. But Richard Cranford's name appeared on the list! she argued a moment later. Surely that made Tony's presence acceptable.

Here, Augusta stepped in. General Parks would be present at the dinner. It would seem very odd—in fact, an outright slight!—if the nephew who lived with him was to be left out. These were all social rules Bella must learn if she hoped to become a hostess on her own shortly. And in England, Charly stuck in, unable to resist, these rules were all much stricter! Bella made no further protest. At least, he had been invited to the ball.

She was to have her reward when they went upstairs to the ballroom. This apartment had never looked lovelier, being lighted, in addition to the chandelier, by wall sconces filled with clusters of tiny wax tapers that would be replaced regularly throughout the evening. Diaphanous pink material hung in loops from the lofty ceiling, creating an impression of tented alcoves along the walls. Potted palms stood in every embrasure, blocking, Charly hoped, exit to the balconies outside.

Tony Marlowe was one of the first arrivals. He mounted the stairs, impeccable in his evening attire, and bowed low before Miss Hanley's wheeled chair. He greeted Charly before turning to Bella and raising her fingers to his lips.

The look that passed between the two caused Charly's heart to sink.

"Your brother has not yet returned?" she asked Tony, quickly breaking in on their intimate moment.

"Haven't seen him in days." With an effort, he dragged his eyes from Bella, radiant in pale rose gauze, and smiled, obviously not heartbroken by that turn of events. "Haven't the faintest notion what he means to do next."

So she still had no help in breaking off this affair. Charly sighed inwardly but had the satisfaction of seeing Tony move away from Bella's side. At least he saw the impropriety of his standing in the receiving line with them!

Relieved from their post at last, Charly and Bella joined the guests, Bella to take the floor very properly on Richard Cranford's arm, and Charly to take up her duties as hostess. These proved not very difficult, for the majority of the guests were well acquainted with one another. She had only to make sure that everyone found partners and that the refreshment tables were constantly refilled.

As the evening drew on, a slight commotion occurred near the door, caused by a late arrival. Looking over, Charly felt her breath catch in her throat in disbelief. Mr. Kevin Marlowe, exquisite in evening dress, had calmly entered the room. How had he the nerve to lower himself to cavort among country bumpkins! And who had the gall to invite him—Tony? With Isabella's permission? She swallowed and took a deep breath, but before she could move to challenge him, her attention was claimed by another guest.

When she looked again, he was nowhere in sight. Not that she was anxious to speak to him, she reminded herself. It would be difficult to know what to say, but she did not have a duty to him as his hostess! She dismissed the matter, turning her attention instead to minding the refreshments.

As she stood overseeing the arrangement of several new trays of tiny rout cakes and pastries, she saw Mr. Marlowe again. This time he was quite near. Suddenly, mischievous sparks lit her eyes and she could not repress a smile. The last time they had met, she had dumped a bucket of water over his head. What would he say now? She nodded to him in greeting. To her surprise, he nodded back and moved at once to her side.

"I fear I am very much a stranger here this evening," he informed her with a bewitching smile. "Which puts me in a quandary. I cannot find our hostess to introduce us."

She blinked, then realized that the admiring gaze that rested on her held not a hint of recognition. Of course! Previously he had only seen her first as a veiled widow, then garbed in Abner's old buckskins with her hair pulled back in a braid and her face streaked with dirt as she struggled with Zephyr. Now the blond ringlets were pulled up high, piled on top of her head with fluffy tendrils framing her face. Her gown was a lavish froth of lace and green satin, and though it was made over from an old one sewn the year of her own come-out, when there was more money for such frivolities, it suited her well. She knew she looked a far cry from the impoverished Mrs. Deane of his memory. He must have thought she had thrown out a lure to a stranger!

"Of course, I admit I am not trying very hard," he continued. "I am quite capable of introducing myself. Kevin Marlowe, completely at your service."

Charly lowered her eyes, pretending a pretty confusion at his forward manners.

"But you do not tell me your name," he coaxed.

"Indeed, sir, I do not know if I should," she responded coyly. She lifted her fan, fluttering it before her face to hide an unholy glee that danced in her eyes.

"Madam Propriety," he murmured, obviously not displeased with her flirtatious manner. "At the very least, grant me your hand for the set that is forming."

Unable to resist, she accepted. Taking her place opposite him, she hoped that others, particularly Jonathan Treadwell, did not notice that she danced. If he did, she would never be free of Jonathan's pesterings that she should do so with him.

"We were fated to meet," Kevin whispered to her as they came together in the movement of the dance.

She looked away, surprised that she blushed, and was glad that the next step required her to circle about him. Hesitantly, she took his hand as they rejoined.

"I feel I dance with a feather," he murmured, his smile a

caress. "I do believe we belong together on the dance floor."

He certainly executed the movements with an extraordinary grace, a sign of that innate balance that made him such an incredible horseman. In spite of her prejudice, she had to admit he could also be very charming. And the most outrageous flirt! Basking in the warm admiration in his eyes and his voice, she could not remember enjoying a dance quite so much before. This was quite another side of Mr. Kevin Marlowe.

Or was it? She responded appropriately to his last sally, but her mind suddenly reverted to cold logic. She looked elegant, she knew, and was obviously one of the chosen few of the beau monde. Had he singled her out because of this? Did he hope to use her as his entrée into the exclusive circle of New York *haut ton*?

"There is that fellow Treadwell," Kevin said suddenly, as they came down the center together.

Charlotte looked up, startled and rather dismayed. She was not ready for her game to come to an end.

"Seem to meet him everywhere I go. He is a merchant, is he not?" he asked, and she confirmed it.

"In England . . ." He broke off, shaking his head as they completed a turn. "Well, it seems odd. Apparently, being in trade holds no stigma here in America."

To her regret, when the dance ended Jonathan came to her side almost at once, ever a dog in the manger.

"Your aunt is asking for you, Mrs. Deane," he said coldly, and offered her his arm.

"Deane . . . !" Kevin Marlowe raised his quizzing glass and regarded her through it. Recognition dawned and his eyes opened wide. "Good God!"

She swept him a mocking curtsy. "Just so, Mr. Marlowe." Accepting Jonathan's arm, she walked off.

"Confounded mushroom!" To her mortification, Jonathan spoke the words in a tone quite audible to Marlowe.

CHAPTER

Eight

*T*he strain of the ball left Charly with a vast longing for the tranquility of her farm. She rose quite late in the morning, and knew that only fresh air would rid her of the headache that threatened to engulf her. Leaving notes for Bella and Aunt Augusta, she sent for old Bruno and her light chaise.

As she ran down the front steps, drawing on her driving gloves, a familiar buggy rounded the corner and pulled up before the house. Silas Hawkes waved as he saw her, and for a moment her heart froze. Now what? But he was smiling.

"Just going out?" he called. "May I offer you an alternative to a somewhat muddy walk?"

"Thank you, no. I was about to drive out to the farm, but that can wait." Her relief was immediate. "Do come in."

He climbed down, hitching his horse at the rail by the kennel, and she led the way back into the drawing room. "How does everything go there?" she asked. "Is all still well?"

"Left old Ben picking up nails," he told her, taking the wing chair she indicated and perching carefully on its edge. "He had both Jim and Henry hard at work, putting them back in a bucket."

He drew his pipe from his pocket and turned it over,

-98-

studying it. Regretfully he replaced it, aware of Augusta Hanley's dislike of tobacco smoke in her rooms. He looked up, sideways, at Charly. "Have you thought any more of selling to me, Mrs. Deane? Your place would be just what I need to round off my own lands. And I'll make you a fair offer."

She shook her head. "I have no intention of selling. That place is a part of me. I could never let it go."

He nodded, understanding her love for her land. "Well, if the choice is ever taken out of your hands, ma'am, keep me in mind. Now I'll not keep you from your journey." He rose. "I've had my say and I'll move along."

They went out into the street together, and he drove off to complete the business that had brought him to New York. Charly's chaise had arrived. She thanked Aunt Augusta's coachman as she got in, and gave Bruno the office.

Ben met her at the farm gate, his face unwontedly serious as he handed Bruno over to Jim. Charly looked at him in sudden alarm.

"Ben, something's happened."

"Nothing we couldn't handle, ma'am." He walked beside her as she hurried toward the stables. "Our prowler came back last night. Jim heard Wind snorting and restless in his box and came down carrying his pitchfork. He saw someone run out the gate, but the thieving rascal was on his horse and away before Jim could catch him."

"What did he do? Ben, did he injure Wind?" A real fear gripped her.

"No, but lucky Jim called me and we took a lantern and looked. You recall that bucket of rusty shoe nails in the barn? Whoever it was had upset it in Wind's paddock. We closed the horse in the box until it was daylight and we could see to pick up the nails. All's well now."

Well! Charly shivered, a cold chill running up her spine. A rusty nail in Wind's foot and tetanus would end his career once and for all!

"We got them up, every last nail," Ben assured her. "The boys fell to like troopers."

Charly thanked him in a rather hollow voice and walked across to the field where Zephyr ran with her new colt.

Deliberate damage—and of potentially the worst kind. She had allowed herself to be lulled into a false sense of security, and now she came down to earth. This time there could be no doubt. She admitted to feeling deeply disturbed, for she could no longer rationalize the strange happenings at the farm. Someone truly wanted her ruined.

Only her promise to escort Bella to an alfresco party that afternoon induced Charly to leave the farm. She arrived back to find her sister already dressed and waiting anxiously. The girl sprang up the moment she entered the front hall.

"Oh, do hurry, Charly! Whatever could have possessed you to go to the farm? No, do not tell me, just go and change your gown!"

This Charly was quite willing to do. At least one of the things that bothered her she could rectify. Jonathan Treadwell's calling Kevin Marlowe a "confounded mushroom," and in his hearing, haunted her. It had been uncalled-for and utterly rude, and she was quite impatient for a chance to apologize for the snobbishness that had its base in sheer jealousy. Marlowe must know by now that there were no such social distinctions in America, and she longed to prove it to him—though why, she could not fathom, unless it was to uphold the integrity of New York's high society.

Apologizing was completely unnecessary, of course. He certainly had recognized Treadwell's remark as a case of the pot calling the kettle black, for he shared Treadwell's toplofty social orientations. He had said so, himself!

Still, it distressed her when the opportunity to set him right on American manners was denied. The evening went by without her so much as glimpsing the irritating Mr. Kevin Marlowe. Prevented from carrying out her intention to apologize for Jonathan, she contented herself with snubbing that gentleman unmercifully.

This state of affairs did not escape the watchful eye of Aunt Augusta. Catching her niece as she set off for her farm the next morning, she took her severely to task.

"Never did I expect to have cause to blush for your manners, my girl," she said sternly.

"And have you now?" Charlotte paused just over the

threshold to the drawing room, regarding her aunt, who sat in her accustomed place near the hearth.

"Your conduct toward Jonathan Treadwell last night was abominable!"

"And so has his been," she responded promptly, a glint of amusement lighting her blue eyes. She came farther into the room and cast her leather driving gloves on a table. "He can be the most vexatious creature! I wonder that you can have been taken in by his cozening ways."

Augusta sighed. "Now what has he done to be placed in your black book?"

"Nothing new to me. This time he has been quite rude to Mr. Kevin Marlowe."

Her aunt emitted a sound that came perilously near a snort. "*That* bothers you? From what you have said, I rather thought it should have ingratiated Jonathan."

Charlotte studied the flickering flames in the cavernous fireplace with unwarranted care. "Oh, it was not the fact that his remark was addressed to *him*; it was that Jonathan involved *me* in his rudeness. He presumes too much, and it is high time he realizes that I am not his for the taking. He behaves as if he owns me! And before you give me that lecture again on how he is my only hope and I am at my last prayers"—here she rounded on Aunt Augusta almost crossly—"let me tell you that I would rather marry Silas Hawkes than Jonathan Treadwell! And . . . I do not intend to marry anyone!" Turning on her heel, she almost ran out of the room, leaving her aunt to watch her with a new, curious gleam in her old eyes.

All seemed well at the farm. Ben and the two boys had divided up the hours so that one of them stood guard at all times, not just on watch from the windows but actually patrolling the fields. All the fences were inspected each morning before the horses were turned out to pasture. Three hours spent in grooming her gray mare and in driving to and from the farm did much to restore Charlotte's worried mind. She returned to New York earlier than she had planned, and as she pulled up before the house, a most unwelcome sight met her gaze. Bella, with no one but the Beautiful Tony accompanying her, came walking blithely down the street.

The girl laughed gaily at something her escort said, glanced up, and froze. She recovered in a moment and tossed her head defiantly. Deliberately, she smiled up into the handsome face of her companion. He had checked also at sight of Charlotte, but Bella dragged him forward to where her sister waited on the walkway for them.

"So, you are returned!" Bella called with a forced airiness.

"As you see," Charly replied, her words cold as ice. "Good afternoon, Mr. Marlowe."

He bowed to her but received no encouragement. After a quick sideways look at Bella's uneasy face, he took his leave of them.

Charly waited until they had entered the house. In the hall, she turned toward the drawing room. This was something that could not be allowed to pass without comment, and it had best not wait.

Bella, without so much as a glance at her sister, walked past her and started up the stairs.

"Bella!" Charly's voice held a decided edge.

The girl stopped, then turned slowly, obviously bracing herself. "Yes?"

"In here, if you please."

Bella seemed on the verge of saying that she did not please, but apparently thought better of it. She flounced down the stairs and into the indicated room.

"This really will not do," Charly told her as soon as she had closed the door behind them. "And don't play the innocent!" she ordered, forestalling Bella's wide-eyed denial. "You know perfectly well what we are talking about. If you continue to walk with Tony Marlowe, without chaperon, you will be labeled fast. And if you show others that unrepentant face, you are ruined for certain!"

"Please, Charly, I know what I am doing."

"I take leave to doubt that. There has already been a deal of gossip. If not for your own sake, then consider poor Aunt Augusta! How can you wish to cause her such embarrassment?"

"But I don't! Oh, why are people so detestable!" Tears started to Bella's eyes. She burst into hysterical sobs and ran from the room, leaving Charly to stare after her in dismay.

By the time she had dressed for a private concert that evening, Charly still had not thought of a way to bring Bella to her senses about her conduct. Her own snubbing of the Beautiful Tony would do no good. For the sake of appearances, she greatly feared she must at least seem complacent. For her to openly declare her opposition—or publicly censor her sister's conduct—would only give rise to more gossip and speculation.

Bella, looking pale and withdrawn, came down the stairs. For once, Aunt Augusta had chosen to accompany them. Jensen called for a chair to take her the few blocks, and Charly, aided by a footman, helped her aunt into the ground floor drawing room at the home of their friends. Bella followed silently. The first person they saw was Tony Marlowe. Forcing a chilly smile to her lips, Charly waited while he came up to them and bowed. Bella murmured a greeting and, to Charly's amazement, turned and walked away.

As Charly stared after her, Bella joined a group of which Richard Cranford was a member. Glancing shyly up at him, she met his eyes for one long moment, then dropped her own demurely. He leaned down, murmured something in her ear, and she giggled, unfurling her fan to hide her face and peeking out at him above it in a coy and teasing manner. Mr. Cranford offered her his arm, and the two strolled off together.

Tony watched this little scene with a darkening brow. Without so much as a nod to Charly or Miss Hanley, he stalked off to a refreshment table where he grabbed a glass of punch. For a moment, Charly feared the contents might find their way into Mr. Cranford's face.

"Now, what is that little minx up to?" Aunt Augusta muttered for Charly's ears alone.

"I sincerely hope she has come to her senses and is making an effort to deny the gossips." Charly frowned. "I only pray she may not be stepping from the fry pan into the fire."

Throughout the rest of the evening, Bella went nowhere near Tony. Instead, she flirted blatantly with Richard Cranford. Even if her motive had not been obvious to her sister, Charly could not have been pleased by such conduct. It did not take Anabel Brougham's drawing her aside to warn her tongues were once more wagging.

"Dear Charlotte, I fear I must, really must, just drop a word in your ear. I am hearing talk of your sister." Miss Brougham sighed with very real anxiety. "Isabella should not spend the entire evening in one gentleman's pocket, especially after she has shown such a decided preference recently for a very different gentleman."

Charly, for once, could think of no retort, which mortified her. Although she felt sure her sister had taken her warning to heart, she had not a doubt that everyone would think Bella used Cranford to make Tony jealous—and from all appearances, the ploy worked to admiration.

Unexpectedly, help arrived. Aunt Augusta, who sat nearby, turned a frosty eye on her crony.

"Let me tell you, Anabel, that both Charlotte and I approve wholeheartedly of a connection with Mr. Richard Cranford." She met and held Miss Brougham's gaze until that lady faltered and suddenly discovered another friend she must greet at once.

"Well done!" Charly murmured.

Augusta Hanley sniffed. "Gossipmongers!" She looked up over her shoulder at Charly. "Anabel is quite right, you know. That silly chit flirts abominably!"

Her old eyes narrowed as she sought out her offending niece. At that moment, Bella stood near the refreshment table while Richard selected delicacies for her. "Now, who would have expected that?" Augusta murmured. "Just look at the way Cranford is positively dancing attendance on a mere chit of a girl!"

"Is that not what you wanted, dear Aunt?" Charly asked, impatiently straightening her skirts.

Augusta ignored her comment. "I have known him any time this past decade, Charly. I saw him frequently before he moved to Philadelphia, and I've seen him several times during the last few years . . . while you've been incarcerated on that farm of yours. And never have I thought him the marrying kind. Showed a decided preference for a very different sort of connection," she added, causing Charly to look at her sharply.

Augusta nodded toward Simone Galbraith, across the room. "Perhaps he feels it is time he settled down—or perhaps he has political ambitions, where a respectable hostess would be an asset." She watched Bella, musing. "If that girl isn't careful," she added severely, "Cranford will see through her tactics. I do not want her driving him away by her shameless antics for young Mr. Marlowe's benefit, not before she and Richard have a chance to get to know each other so that he may fix his interest."

Charly was not pleased with this suggestion. She wanted Bella to marry for love—though not Tony Marlowe! Certainly, Richard Cranford was every inch the gentleman, an entertaining companion, a very suitable husband in every worldly respect, but she could not feel he truly loved Bella. She eyed the two closely, noting each seemed bent on fascinating the other. He admired Bella, certainly, and seemed to like her very well, but Charly could detect none of the signs of a gentleman in the violent throes of love.

She gave herself a shake. She was becoming a hopeless romantic, like Anabel Brougham! What should concern her was Bella's happiness, and certainly Richard Cranford would secure that. He would always be kind and considerate, and that was worth a great deal more than a fleeting passion that would die with her youth.

Even after carrying these thoughts to bed with her, Charly was not prepared when, as she finished her breakfast the following morning, Jensen entered the sunny parlor to announce that Mr. Richard Cranford was below and desired private speech with her. She went down to him at once, and found him pacing the length of the drawing room.

"What can I do for you?" she asked as she went forward, extending her hand.

He took it and bowed low. He made an excellent leg, she noted, approving.

"To be honest," he began with a smile that transformed

his homely face, "I did not know whether I should speak to you or Miss Hanley. I am not sure which of you is Miss Isabella's guardian."

"I am," Charly said, suddenly sinking into a chair. His words could have only one meaning.

"Then I have come to beg your permission to pay my addresses to your sister."

"I . . . that is . . ." She broke off, confused. "Oh, please, do be seated. What can I say? I . . . I fear Bella is still too young to be thinking of marriage."

"You might say that I am too old," Richard said candidly, "especially for a chit of Isabella's age. But I rather think we would rub along tolerably well." An amused glint lit his eyes as he spoke.

At this unfortunate moment, Bella stuck her head into the drawing room, saw Richard and came in, all smiles. "Why, what brings you here this morning?"

"You," he responded.

Bella laughed. "How gallant! You will put me to the blush."

"By all means," he responded. "You do it quite adorably."

Bella did blush then, and giggled like the youngster she still was.

Richard turned to Charly. "If I might have a word alone with Bella?" he asked.

Charly hesitated. She would first like a chance to speak to Bella, but perhaps this might be best after all. Nodding, she withdrew from the room.

It was not long before Bella joined her, strangely subdued. "My first proposal of marriage!" The girl spoke casually, trying to treat it lightly. "Only imagine! And I am barely turned eighteen!"

"What did you tell him?"

"Why, no, of course. Not like that . . . I mean, I told him I was very conscious of the honor he did me, and so forth, but that I . . . I do not feel ready to enter marriage as yet." She looked down at the hand clenched tightly in her lap. "I . . . I do not think I offended him."

"Or wounded him?" Charly asked dryly.

Bella's startled gaze flew to her sister. "Do you think . . . ?

No, he did not seem in the least dismayed, I am sure of it! We parted friends."

Charly, watching her sister, saw that her words had disturbed the girl. It must never have entered her mind that her using Richard might cause him to offer for her! Perhaps his precipitate proposal would be good for Bella. So far, she had been thinking of no one but herself—and Tony.

But if Bella had been upset by Richard Cranford's offer, Aunt Augusta was doubly so by the refusal. No sooner had she learned of her niece's ruinous action than she sent for General Parks.

"You must tell Richard not to despair," she begged her old friend. "Bella is but a foolish child who has not seen enough of the world yet. It is all the fault of her having lived isolated for so long with no one but Charlotte and all those horses." She looked earnestly up into the kindly face opposite her. "Bella is not yet ready for marriage. But you must encourage Richard to hope. Tell him that he spoke too soon. She was frightened, perhaps unsure of her suitability for the position of a wife for such a man as he. He must try again, after giving Bella time to find her feet."

The general took her agitated hands between his own. "You may be sure I shall tell him. But to tell truth, I am surprised the boy offered. I had hoped, of course. Damme, you know how much I would welcome a connection with your family. Just never really thought Richard wanted to settle down."

The proposal had one positive effect on Bella. After studiously avoiding her sister all day, Bella suddenly came to Charly's room while she dressed for dinner. For once, they were to dine at home. Bella cast herself across the bed and watched her sister's reflection in the mirror as Charly brushed out her long hair.

"Did you receive many proposals?" she asked suddenly. She rolled over onto her back and stared up at the ceiling. "It was all so long ago, when you came out. I was only ten. I cannot really remember. But was there not some gentleman to whom you were partial?"

Charly hesitated. "No," she said at last, and even to herself her voice sounded wistful. "I received two offers," she went on hurriedly. "Quite unacceptable, I assure you. I think Pappa was at his wits' end when he met Abner and arranged everything with him."

"A man nearer his own age than yours." Bella sighed. "I wonder what it would be like to receive an offer from the . . . from a man you loved . . ."

Charly bit her lip. She could only be glad Tony Marlowe was not making any proposals—decent or otherwise. He had certainly not asked anyone's permission to pay his addresses. Nor was he likely to, she realized, and for a very good reason. He intended to return to England and marry into the nobility.

"You should not hope too much for Tony to propose," she said forthrightly. "He has a life in England after all, one where an American bride might well be a hindrance."

Bella flushed. "That would not weigh with Tony. The only reason he has not spoken is that he must first get his brother's approval. Kevin controls the purse strings, you know!" She jumped off the bed and ran out of the room.

Charly stared after her, distressed. To her, that seemed a very lame excuse. Kevin would never give his permission for this marriage. Uneasily, she suspected that Tony counted on this to keep him free of a serious entanglement.

When she finally went downstairs to dinner, she was forced to the conclusion that her well-meant words had done more harm than good. Belligerent and withdrawn, Bella would have little to do with her sister and as soon as the meal drew to a close, retired to her chamber.

For Charly, this was harder to bear than anything else. The sisters had always been so close; it struck her almost as a physical pain to see Bella turn away from her. Nor did she dare leave town to seek solace from her horses. In her current mood, Bella might well do anything.

Kevin Marlowe, seated in the coffee room at the Tontine, found himself subject to an odd mood as he sipped at a large tankard of ale. His entire impression of Mrs. Charlotte Deane had undergone a radical change, a change that left him uncertain of his own attitude. Ever since the evening of Isabella Hanley's birthday ball, his usually logical mind had taken erratic turnings to remembrances of golden curls, mischievous blue eyes, and a thoroughly charming face. Who would ever have believed the female was such a beauty?

When she had smiled up at him, one corner of her mouth had gone up farther than the other, giving a tip-tilted look that was altogether delightful. It was not much of a tilt, one had to really look close to see it—and he realized he must have been looking very closely indeed. How, when he studied that lovely face as they danced, had he failed to recognize her? Uncomfortably, he knew he had never really looked at her while he considered her to be beneath his notice. It was a shock to discover that here in America she was actually his social superior! A confounded mushroom, that merchant had called him! He grinned suddenly, once more reliving his encounter with Mrs. Deane. It was, in fact, one in the eye for Petrucchio. There was more to this Kate than he had suspected.

Once more the urge to bring her to heel took hold on him. He had never failed to tame the most spirited filly. Would the same methods work on a woman? Suddenly there was nothing he wanted more than to try.

To Charly's complete astonishment, Kevin Marlowe arrived the following morning to pay her a call. She stared at him for a moment, torn between surprise at his visit and the effect of the most charming smile that had ever been directed at her. Recovering, she took the hand he offered, then gestured for him to take a chair in her aunt's drawing room.

"I have come to suggest a truce," he said as he waited to be seated until she sat down herself. "I will grant you Tony's lack of discretion. A young addlepate, by all means. Now stay in your chair. I did not come here to quarrel with you but to invite you to ride with me this afternoon into the countryside." He smiled again, so like his brother Tony that the effect was staggering. "I can supply two excellent horses, borrowed from the livery stable, if you have not a mount in town."

She blinked, utterly undone by his sudden and unexpected friendliness. In truth, she told herself, she had not ridden in weeks and would like nothing more than a long gallop. Perhaps she could use the time to get on better terms with Kevin Marlowe and induce him to assist her in breaking up their siblings' affair in a manner that would hurt Bella as little as possible. And though she was loath to admit it, she very much wanted to watch her Compleat Horseman ride.

But dare she leave her troublesome sister? Yes. For once, Bella should be quite safe. She had promised to go to the subscription library with Miss Nidbury to bring back *Ormond* for Aunt Augusta. And as their aunt had issued orders that she was not to return without a copy of Mrs. Radcliff's *Udolpho*, and the latest issue of the ''Gentlemen and Ladies' Town and Country Magazine,'' Bella should be quite safe for some time. Unable to resist the temptation, Charly accepted.

When Kevin called for her a few hours later, Charly was waiting for him, attired in her most becoming—and favorite— outfit, a riding habit of rose-colored velvet and a round brown beaver hat with pink ostrich plumes that curled down into her gold ringlets. The expression in his dark eyes as they traveled over her was all that she could have hoped for—more, in fact, for she wanted no liaison with Kevin Marlowe!

She allowed him to throw her up into the saddle. As she settled her skirts about her knee, she watched him out of the corner of her eye as he swung easily up onto his own mount. He looked as if he had almost been born on a horse's back. Never before had she seen anything as naturally graceful as the way he moved with the animal, so completely at one with it that he needed no visible signals for control.

Both horses were fresh and eager, which pleased her. He had done her the courtesy of not underrating her skill at riding. Together, they set off down the crowded street, keeping the animals to a dignified trot. They would not be able to give them free rein until they were clear of the city traffic and beyond the flat stone paving.

As they rode in silence through the busy streets, Charly kept a surreptitious eye on Kevin Marlowe. She was herself a superb horsewoman, but she suspected she could learn a few things from him. Not that she was about to admit it!

"I see you are quite expert at handling your mount," he remarked as they at last reached open territory. There was a pronounced gleam of admiration in the eyes that rested on her. He looked her over slowly, taking in every detail of the becoming riding habit. The appreciation deepened and she blushed, turning her face away, suddenly nervous. Surely no gentleman would inspect a lady's charms in so direct a manner!

"Tony," he remarked conversationally, "is a young fool. He has picked the wrong sister to seduce."

Charly stiffened. "If that means you think either of us would welcome such advances, then you are very much mistaken! May I take leave to inform you, Mr. Marlowe, that I consider your brother an unprincipled libertine?"

"Of course, you may inform me of anything you wish. But are you quite certain a lady should use such expressions?" Once more that devastating smile left her shaken. She rallied at once.

"Oh, I need not scruple to guard my tongue with you, I am sure! And since you have given me leave, I shall tell you right now that nothing—absolutely nothing!—would ever induce me to countenance an alliance between my sister and your beastly brother! Even if his intentions were honorable, which I cannot believe! Why do you not take him and go back where you came from?"

Kevin merely shrugged. "Force will not grant his compliance. The infatuation will soon run its course. And in the meantime, I find I am in no hurry to leave America." He changed the subject abruptly. "Why do you persist in this foolish undertaking of trying to breed superior race horses?"

"To support ourselves, of course," she replied, a trifle surprised at her own candor. "If I had not the farm, we should be obliged to hang on my aunt's sleeve, and that is something we will never do! My hopes are all on Bella . . ." She broke off, vibrant color flooding her cheeks as she realized what she had almost said. Deep down, she had secretly counted on the lovely Bella to make an advantageous marriage and save them both. Why, she was no better than Kevin Marlowe!

He glanced at her, noting her silence but seemingly not the reason for it. "Have you no relatives to take care of you?" he demanded roughly.

"My father's sister is our only near relation."

"Then you must put yourselves in her charge. Surely, you realize that single females cannot reside alone without becoming the targets for every loose fish in town as well as the gossipmongers."

"Only when 'loose fish,' as you term them, make it their object to trifle with the poor females!"

"When he receives every encouragement from the girl," he responded, having no illusions about which "loose fish" they spoke, "you can hardly blame him. If a female throws out an obvious lure, she should expect to catch a loose fish on her hook."

"Not if she is accustomed to meeting only *gentlemen*!" She threw the words at him.

"True, but then a *lady* would not find herself in such a position, would she?"

Charly gripped her reins, causing her horse to sidle uneasily. "I believe we understand each other tolerably well," she said through clenched teeth. "I see no need for further discussion on this . . . or any other . . . topic."

Unexpectedly, he grinned. "That's my Kate!"

Now what did he mean by that? She tossed her head. "My name is Charlotte, but I do not believe I have given you permission to use it."

"As you say." Feigning meekness, he rode up beside her. "Let us stick to pleasanter topics than our aggravating siblings. Tell me, what is the name of this delightful stream we are splashing through?" He shook his head sadly. "It seems I am doomed to get wet whenever we meet. It is my fate."

Charlotte, startled into a giggle at the memory of their encounter in Zephyr's stall, recovered her good temper. The rest of the ride, amazingly, passed in the best of humor. It almost seemed as though Mr. Kevin Marlowe was bent on gaining entry to her good graces, for what motive she could not discern. On her part, though never had she felt quite so in charity with that gentleman, she maintained a cool front. She would not give an inch to the philandering Marlowe brothers, be they ever so charming. The sooner they left New York, the better for her peace of mind.

CHAPTER
Nine

*T*he following morning, Aunt Augusta called Charly as she was about to set forth on a visit. Bella, it seemed, had just left for the New York Society Library but had forgotten to take *Udolpho* back with her. Would her dearest Charly take it?

Glad of the excuse to forego a boring social duty, Charly decided to walk the five blocks to the corner of Liberty and Nassau streets. As she entered the building, she found Miss Nidbury wandering from room to room, looking for her charge.

"She often disappears," Niddy assured her, smiling. "I usually find her in a quiet corner, reading. Dear child."

Her sister had never been bookish in her life! Suddenly filled with a dreadful sense of foreboding, Charly began a serious search. She should have guessed something was afoot when Bella nobly offered to exchange books and journals for Aunt Augusta nearly every day. She had thought—or perhaps wanted to believe—it to be gratitude for all that their aunt did in sponsoring a season for her.

Finally, as she had feared, she discovered Bella secreted in an almost hidden alcove with Tony. As she looked in, he was holding her hands. Bella, hearing the footsteps, looked up at Charly and gasped.

Tony cleared his throat. "Mrs. Deane," he began uneasily. "It is not at all what it appears! We met by sheer chance, and—"

"Sheer chance? In this out-of-the way little alcove? You amaze me!"

He had the grace to flush. "I realize it must look incriminating, but—"

"If you realize it, then I am shocked you could have done anything so surely injurious to Bella's reputation! Only think what would have been the result had anyone other than I found you!" She swallowed hard, for she found she was trembling. "Now, if you please, Mr. Marlowe, it will be best if you leave before you are seen by someone else."

He threw a look of mute apology to Bella, sketched a hasty bow to Charlotte, and departed. She could only hope that his obvious reluctance to leave lay in having some qualms at deserting Bella to face the music alone.

Charly and Bella were left facing one another. "I hope you realize that you and Tony have behaved in the most reprehensible manner!" Charly finally said. She watched her sister's flushed countenance. "There is no need for secrecy! If his intentions are honorable, he has only to come to the house!"

"Oh, you do not understand!" Bella wailed, dissolving into tears. "You have never been in love! What can you possibly know of the persecutions we undergo!"

"Persecutions!" Charly exclaimed, indignant. "But I have just told you—"

"From Tony's brother! And you may *say* Tony is welcome at home, but I know he is not. You are selfish, Charly! You ... you want to destroy my only chance for happiness! You are afraid Tony will take me home to England and leave you all alone with nothing but your silly horses!"

Charly closed her eyes and counted to twenty, very slowly. She knew who had planted that idea in Bella's mind. The little fool believed everything the Beautiful Tony said! Without another word, Charly led Bella back to the entrance of the library, where they found Miss Nidbury peacefully waiting, oblivious of everything.

* * *

As she dressed for a dinner party that evening, Charly reviewed their conversation. She thought of several choice epithets she could have applied to both the Marlowe brothers, and there were a number of things she would dearly have loved to say to Kevin Marlowe, in terms that would undoubtedly have caused Aunt Augusta to abuse her soundly for possessing such a shocking vocabulary. The very nerve of Mr. Kevin Marlowe, to say his brother had chosen to seduce the wrong sister!

She stopped in the act of sliding a hairpin into a long golden ringlet. Seduce the wrong sister. Her eyes opened wide as she stared at herself in the mirror. She was still quite attractive and far more knowledgeable in the art of flirtation than her little sister. Could this prove a solution? Could she possibly steal Tony from her?

Bella's heart might be seriously involved, but that of the Beautiful Tony was another matter. If he merely trifled with Bella, at the expense of her innocence . . . Let Bella see for herself that he was nothing more than a loose fish—to use his own brother's expression!

She added the finishing touches to her toilette, but her mind was far from the evening's entertainment. Bella, sweet innocent that she was, would be shocked if she realized what Charlotte believed to be Tony's intentions. So far, Charly had been wise enough to do no more than just hint, knowing her besotted sister would never believe ill of Tony. But if Bella caught him trying to seduce her own sister, she would have to accept the truth!

Still, she shied away from putting such a plan into action. The very idea was repellent! But Bella's happiness meant a great deal to her, and she would not have the unprincipled Tony wreak havoc on her sister's heart. She had no choice. She must break this affair off before any more damage was done. And much as she hated the idea, she feared there was only one way. If Kevin Marlowe thought her attractive, perhaps she could do it. She had never tried to take a man from another woman, but with the stakes so high, she had to make the attempt.

The needs of business required her presence at the farm— and required her to put the problem of Tony aside for a day.

She prepared for the drive, leaving Bella in the care of Aunt Augusta. Reluctantly, she had told Miss Hanley of the clandestine meeting in the library, and her indignant aunt swore not to let Bella out of her sight until Charly's return.

"Fool girl! Does she think to let him compromise her and thus compel him to make an offer?"

Charly sighed. "I have no idea. To be sure, the little idiot has tried everything else. She will have told him of Cranford's proposal, and if that did not do the trick, I fail to see why she continues to hope." But hope Bella did, and Charly could see nothing for it but to carry out her drastic plan. Tomorrow she'd think about it, for now business took precedence.

She worked late that evening in her small study at the farm, and began again the next day after breakfast. How could her bills amount to so much?

She set down her cup of late morning tea and frowned at the page of figures in her account book. The bottom line left much to be desired. With heroic effort, she kept her mind from Zephyr, who ran free and unconcerned in the pasture with her colt. At least another hour's work lay ahead of her before she could go out to watch them.

She closed her eyes. Somehow, there must be a simple solution to the demands of the tradesmen—and one that did not involve marriage with Jonathan Treadwell! With a deep sigh, she began to go over her figures once more on the forlorn hope that she might have made a mistake.

She was so engrossed that she failed to hear the sounds of an approaching carriage in her lane. The knocker, vigorously applied on the front door, finally penetrated, but she gave it no heed. Not, in fact, until the rapping sound had been repeated twice more did it rouse her, and she realized Myra must be busy in the kitchen preparing dinner for Ben and the boys.

Charly rose to answer the door herself. To her amazement, Pieter Van Bleek stood there, looking absurdly out of place in the country surroundings in his elegant town dress.

He raised disapproving eyebrows. "You answer your own door, Mrs. Deane?"

"Only when my housekeeper is busy." Charly stepped

aside to allow him to enter, on her guard, mistrusting the note in his voice.

"I have heard disturbing news, most disturbing indeed," he said, coming straight to the point as she led him to the drawing room. He met her eyes squarely. "You have lost the stallion which provided the foundation for your program."

Charly sank into a chair, suddenly weak. With an effort, she kept her countenance from reflecting her stunned shock.

"I came to see for myself if this was true," he went on in tones of doom as he took the seat opposite her. "If this is the case, I fear I will have no choice but to foreclose at once."

She swallowed, forcing her voice to cooperate. "You forget, sir, you gave me six months!"

He frowned. "Surely this cancels any agreement we may have had."

She shook her head with more firmness than certainty. "That it does not! I have the signed paper, and I shall hold you to the letter of it. I will find another stallion, rest assured." She watched him closely, but his countenance gave away nothing. She continued with more confidence than she felt. "In the meantime, as you know, I have a two-year-old entered at Maidenhead who will prove the excellence of my bloodline. I fully expect, on the strength of his winning, to sell my yearlings for enough to pay off the remainder of Abner's debt."

"Do you mean to tell me that I am to wait for my money? To accept, as a guarantee, the paces of an untried colt?" He shook his head, a contemptuous twist in his thin lips. "Really, Mrs. Deane, I must protest."

Charly stood her ground. "I shall hold you to our agreement." She rose, her defiance shining in her eyes. "My land, not my stallion, stood collateral."

Mr. Van Bleek also came to his feet and took a rapid turn about the room. He stopped suddenly and glared at her. "You may be within your legal rights to do so, ma'am, but it would be foolish beyond permission! I beg of you, in your own best interests, give up before you are totally bankrupt. When Mr. Treadwell informed me of your misfortune—"

"What?"

"Mr. Jonathan Treadwell, a business acquaintance of mine. I encountered him first thing this morning at the Tontine Coffee House, and he happened to mention your predicament to me."

"Jonathan!" A cold anger swelled within her. Jonathan Treadwell had much to answer for!

His brows drew together. "This extension was given entirely against my better judgment. I should never have let Marlowe talk me into it."

Charly froze, staring at him. All her notions of his enmity were crashing about her. He was her benefactor, not the odious snob she believed him. She attempted to regain her scattered wits.

Van Bleek stood before her, seemingly a long way off. In the turmoil of the reversal of her feelings, she felt oddly divorced from the present. Why did her heart suddenly sing? Why should this removal of the foundation for her carefully nurtured dislike of Kevin Marlowe cause such a sensation of relief?

She realized Van Bleek waited for her to speak, and said the first thing that came into her head.

"You . . . you must excuse me, Mr. Van Bleek. I have a great deal to think about this morning. Be assured, you will be repaid. I . . . I have five months left, and I intend to use them."

She led the way to the door, and he had little choice but to follow her. She opened it for him and he paused on the threshold, taking her hand.

"As I said, you are being foolish beyond permission, Mrs. Deane. Legally, you may hold me to the agreement, though I strongly advise you to stop now, while you can still sell off your horses and possibly the property for enough to pay your debt and still be able to live until your remarriage."

"My . . . remarriage!" Why did her thoughts fly at once to Kevin Marlowe?

"Yes, Mr. Treadwell informs me that splendid occasion is not far distant. May I wish you both happy."

That did it. Charly came back down to earth with a thud. Treadwell again! She drew her slight frame to its fullest height. "Good morning," she said in frozen tones, not trusting herself to say more.

Fury with Jonathan filled her as she slammed the door closed after Van Bleek. Oh, he had a great deal to answer for. What a bumbling fool he was! Did he hope to win her over by such tactics? Or was his purpose to force her into the position of having no other choice? He was far too quick to take advantage of her misfortune. And to discuss her affairs—and her!—in a place devoted exclusively to men and their business pursuits was unforgiveable! He had bandied her name once too often. If he truly loved her, as he claimed, why was he not helping in some way? How, she didn't know, but the least he could do was offer! Tony, a mere acquaintance, had helped lay traps when they had feared the prowler.

This was a fortunate thought, for it caused her to forget her anger for a minute as the soggy figure of Kevin Marlowe, standing in the puddle under the light of Ben's lantern, rose in her mind. Well, there were some compensations in this unpleasant business—one very large one. A warm happiness filled her even as she knew it to be irrational. So he was not her enemy. That did not make him a friend.

Restless, she donned a shawl and headed out past the barns, to where Zephyr and her foal played and grazed in the back pasture. As she leaned on the rail fence, Silas Hawkes drove along his lane on the other side and raised his hand in greeting. She waved back, and saw him cast an envious glance out over her land before going on around to her front gate.

His land was really too small for his needs. This was not the first time she had seen him eyeing her property wistfully. He had not nearly enough pasture.

A few minutes later, Silas appeared around the corner of her barn. He came to the fence and joined her, gazing across at her horses rather than at her.

"You look disturbed," was all he said.

Charlotte shook her head. "Merely thoughtful. It is peaceful watching the foal play."

"And a fine field to do it in, too." Silas gave her one of

his sideways glances. "Be glad to take it off your hands, you just say the word."

"Thank you, but no." She tried to smile, but this came too hard on Van Bleek's visit. She felt as though everyone joined to force her into a corner, which made her want to fight all the harder. Silas, Van Bleek, Jonathan, Tony Marlowe—why did the removal of Kevin Marlowe from this list seem to mitigate all the others?

Silas broke in on her thoughts. "Can't help but wonder if that Summer Wind of yours is large enough at his age for this race meet," he said with a shade too much casualness. "Has to carry weight, you know."

"Ben is small."

"True, but the horse is barely two years of age." Silas shook his head. "Still, I wish you the best of luck. Good day to you, Mrs. Deane." He walked off.

She stared after him, a victim of unwelcome speculation. Her being ruined would work out very well for Silas Hawkes. And he had not told her Storm was killed deliberately. He must have known . . .

At that moment, Ben came out of the near barn and she called to him. Setting aside the pitchfork he carried, he crossed over to join her.

"Ben, who else knew about the powder burns on Summer Storm? Have you told anyone?"

"Of course not, Mrs. Deane." He looked as affronted as if she had just accused him of treason.

"Did the boys know?" she pursued.

"They'll not speak of it."

"But Silas did?"

"Oh, yes. He was there when I first saw them. Mentioned them, and he bent down and had a look, too."

But he had not told her. And there was a good chance he had not spoken of it to anyone else, either. It would not serve his purposes if he wanted her land. "So, basically, no one knows but we three, and the boys." She spoke her thoughts aloud.

"Possibly, ma'am."

Charly sighed. Suddenly, it was vital to her that the truth not come out. If Mr. Van Bleek learned someone was intentionally trying to ruin her, he would do everything in his power to foreclose. Who knew what pressure he might bring to bear to protect his investment? And she had enough problems at the moment! Best he never came to know someone was on his side. Unless it was a minion of his own causing her problems! She would have to swear the others to secrecy. She turned to Ben. "Let's try to keep anyone else from finding out."

Ben nodded. "We're keeping up the night watches, Mrs. Deane. I've divided the dark hours between the three of us, and we each carry one of the cowbells. At the slightest sign of anyone snooping about, the clamor will raise the others. And I'm keeping my loaded musket by my bed."

Charlotte could not be at ease, but she had promised to chaperon Bella to a dinner that evening. As she drove Bruno back to town, her thoughts turned from one set of problems to another. Since her sister's eighteenth birthday, the girl's attitude had undergone a drastic change, and Charly laid it at Tony Marlowe's door. No longer did she run to her adored elder sister with every little enthusiasm or sorrow. She had become a young lady overnight—and one secretive and distrustful. A female of her advanced years, she seemed to believe, should no longer need advice or chaperonage. Charly, sincerely missing Bella's impulsive affection, hoped that this phase would soon pass.

The dinner party proved more elaborate than Charly expected. As they entered their hostess's drawing room, she was surprised to see so many people present, though only one caught her eye. For her, Kevin Marlowe, immaculate in a coat of dark blue velvet, dominated the company. She tried to look away, willing herself not to notice his presence.

It proved impossible. He stood in one corner, involved in what appeared to be a delightful conversation with Mrs. Simone Galbraith. He might not be as handsome as Tony, but he obviously held an allure for the ladies.

As if sensing her eyes on him, he looked up and smiled in a taunting manner as he saw her. Excusing himself to his companion, he strode over to join her.

Bracing herself, Charly forced a polite smile to her lips.

She had not seen him since learning that he approved the short extension on her loan, and soft color flooded her cheeks as she realized she must thank him—and apologize for her antagonism. Of a certainty he would enjoy her discomfiture. But she wasn't ready to face him! Before she could stop, she blurted out her first thought. "How come you to be here?"

It was rude, and she flushed, but he accepted it as a normal opening gambit.

"Tony brought me. He apparently is in very good odor with our hostess and therefore allowed to include a mushroom among her distinguished guests."

He did indeed seem to take a perverse delight in her embarrassment, for his eyes glinted with suppressed amusement as he bowed over her hand.

"I have only just learned that you recommended the extension to Mr. Van Bleek," she plunged in. She kept her voice cool, as if divorcing herself from her words. "I must thank you."

"No, must you? Do you not find it difficult?" he asked with solicitous concern. An overwhelming impulse to giggle at his absurdity got the better of her, and he smiled his approval. "Yes, that is much better," he assured her. "You should laugh more often."

She pulled herself together, refusing to succumb to the temptation of becoming one of his numerous flirts. It was a talent the brothers shared, and while she was grateful to him, she had no intention of falling victim to his disturbing charm.

"I do thank you," she informed him with a measure of reserve. "Though I wish one of you might have told me earlier! You have allowed me to resent you needlessly!"

"Well, it was hardly for me to tell you." Kevin favored her with a beguiling smile.

"No, I suppose you found it more entertaining to be forever at daggers drawn!"

"Oh, I am sure we would manage that anyway," came the prompt response.

In spite of herself, she laughed again, then moved hurriedly on. A flirtation with him could be quite appealing.

But his intentions were merely to amuse himself—and at the lady's expense! Not for a moment could she allow herself to forget his unflattering opinion of Americans in general and the Hanley sisters in particular. Let him enjoy the likes of that free and easy Galbraith female!

To her intense relief, she found she was seated at the far end of the dinner table from either of the Marlowe brothers. Her sister, she noted with dismay, sat almost opposite Tony. Bella's training was too strict to allow her to speak to anyone other than the gentleman on either side of her, but the languishing looks she cast at her handsome swain were enough to make Charly long to give her a tongue-lashing. The sooner she could break this up, the better for her heedless sister's reputation! But could she lure Tony away? She had to try.

As the meal drew to a close, the ladies retired to the drawing room. Bella, as if sensing Charly's disapproval, seated herself with two of her friends and pointedly turned her back on her sister. Charlotte was forced to bide her time and make polite conversation with several of her aunt's friends.

When the gentlemen rejoined the ladies, Tony paused in the doorway, threw a casual glance about the room, then strolled up to Charly in a manner so offhand as to be unbelievable. Instantly she became suspicious. Bella's back remained turned toward her, so she could gain no clue from that quarter.

Tony beamed down at her. A less prepared female would have melted on the spot. Charly merely smiled back, unmoved—except by the nagging resemblance to his brother Kevin's more charming moments.

He took the seat at her side. "I have come to beg your permission to visit Deane Farm." He adopted the expression of a hopeful puppy, found, to his surprise, that for once it failed, and instead tried a boyish grin. "Bella has told me that Summer Wind is being trained on a quarter-mile stretch along the verge of your lane and I would love to watch him run."

"I believe you saw him at his best just running free in the pasture," Charly countered.

"He was certainly a beauty there," Tony agreed. "But I have heard so much about his potential from Bella, I can hardly wait to see his paces under saddle."

Charly blinked. Here, of his own accord, he offered her the opening she needed! What was she thinking of, trying to discourage him? His love of horses might well provide her chance to captivate him and lure him away from her sister just long enough to discredit him in Bella's eyes!

Swallowing her own feelings, she bestowed a brilliant smile on him. "Wind is everything Bella has said. Of course you must see for yourself! How can I resist showing him off? We will be quite happy to see you . . . anytime you choose to come."

In her mind, she donned the rose-colored habit and prepared to be at her most provocative. But a few moments of panic blurred the picture. It had been many years since she flirted with a young man. Could she get away with it? She could only be glad that his beautiful looks left her unmoved. Now, if she were forced to play this trick on his brother Kevin . . . She shut off that line of thought, thankful that the elder Mr. Marlowe did not come into this.

"Would tomorrow morning be all right?" Tony watched her eagerly.

"It would, indeed. Until then?" Charly rose. "If Bella and I are to drive home in the morning, I need to see that she gets to sleep early. I will bid you a good night."

She crossed the room and laid one hand gently on her sister's shoulder. Bella turned, and the dancing lights died from her eyes as she beheld her sister.

"What is it?" she demanded.

"If you do not mind, dearest, I would like us to go home early this evening. I plan to leave for the farm by eight, if possible."

Bella shrugged. "Surely there is no need for me to accompany you."

"Of course not. I can show Tony Marlowe around by myself." She realized her error even as she spoke. Now Bella would come along, and she really needed to be alone if she was to attempt to intrigue Tony. Stupid!

"T... Tony?" Bella spun back to face her, her eyes wide.

"He wishes to see Wind in a training session. But you may stay home with Aunt Augusta, if you would rather," she suggested, but without much hope.

Bella most definitely would rather not. They left the party shortly, and Bella did not make so much as a murmur about going straight to bed. It did surprise Charly somewhat, though, when she descended the stairs to the breakfast parlor the following morning and found her slugabed sister already there before her, dressed and ready to depart.

"Do you know?" the girl began as she scrambled up into the chaise a short time later. "I have not worn my riding habit of late. Do you suppose it will need pressing?" All animosity forgotten, she bubbled in her excitement.

Charly turned old Bruno onto Broad Way and coerced him into a trot. "What, do you mean you actually intend to watch the training?" There was a light, teasing note in her voice, but she felt an undercurrent of annoyance. Bella had never been one to brave dirt or tedious hours, and she had half counted on having the time alone with Tony after all. Bella's presence would be a complication, for she could not have her sister see her openly throwing out lures to Tony, for then the blame would fall on her, not him. She would have to concentrate on his love of racing and talk "horse," not stressing her femininity. Of course, that did not preclude her being at her most charming, perhaps even somewhat inviting.

They arrived at the farm barely an hour before Tony, but both sisters used the time to advantage. Bella, radiant in her sapphire blue habit, with her golden curls just peeping out from beneath her plumed beaver hat, descended the stairs only moments before they heard Tony's horse canter into the yard. Charly, down before her, went to the door herself, thus gaining a moment to greet their visitor warmly.

Tony swung down from his horse, tossed the reins to Jim, and came up the steps. He paused just below Charly, his eyes wide with admiration at the perfect picture she made in the habit that reflected a dusky rose on cheeks brushed by curling plumes. Charlotte felt her confidence, which had been wavering badly, soar.

Bella hurried out in her wake, and the three of them proceeded at once to the lane, where Ben had already put Wind through his warmup. The morning session went well; Charlotte nodded with pleasure. Wind, a beautiful sight at any time, chose to be at his most impressive, making each start with a surge of energy that drew a soft whistle from Tony.

"What I wouldn't give . . ." Tony breathed. Impulsively, he turned to Charly. "Let me ride him, just for one run. Please!"

Charly hesitated. She would certainly win his gratitude. But would it be safe? Wind did not take kindly to any rider other than Ben. A new idea occurred to her. If Tony was thrown before two ladies, the embarrassment, after all his great talk, might well cool Bella's ardor.

She called to Ben, and he reluctantly turned over the reins. Nervous, Charly leaned on the rails next to the excited Bella, watching, dreading the possible outcome. If Tony was hurt . . .

But Wind responded well to Tony's hands. Bella jumped up and down, ecstatic, as the pair flew by and then slowed to a trot at the end of the sprint.

"Oh, Charly! I vow I have never seen a horseman his like!"

Charlotte held her tongue. Mentally contrasting him with his brother, she found Tony sadly wanting. He was graceful, certainly, but he lacked the absolute perfection of Kevin.

Tony rode up and slid down from the saddle, patting the animal's neck. "He's everything you said!" he exclaimed, enthusiastic. "Please, let me ride him in the race! We can do wonders together!" He tried to stroke Wind's head, but the horse shook off his hand.

"No," Charly said, but this time she let her tone be less definite than before.

Ben spat on the ground. "Now, don't you go even considering it, Mrs. Deane!" he declared. "That horse will be excited and high-strung enough without strange hands on his bridle. This race is too important to risk, and well you know it!" He almost snatched the reins back from Tony and led the horse off.

Charlotte managed a convincing laugh. "Dear Ben. He really knows that horse better than anyone, even me. But don't let this put you off, Tony." She considered fluttering her eyelashes, then discarded the idea. "You may come visit us again, whenever you choose."

They returned to the house, where Myra had prepared tea and refreshments. Charly immediately sent for ale for Tony, coyly remarking that gentlemen always preferred something stronger after riding. Tony endorsed that opinion enthusiastically, and when he rode off at last, nothing could have surpassed the friendliness of the mood all around.

Bella stood waving until he headed his mount onto the lane, then turned to give her sister an impulsive hug. "Oh, Charly, it has been the most pleasant morning, has it not? And Tony is . . . is so . . . so marvelous!"

That was not quite the word that Charly would have used to describe him, but she agreed, thankful to have Bella her sweet self once again. On the whole, she was satisfied with the morning's work. Bella suspected nothing as yet, and the groundwork had been well laid. If her conscience gave her a twinge, she ignored it. It was for Bella's own good.

CHAPTER

Ten

Tony burst unceremoniously into his brother's rooms at the Tontine just as Kevin returned from lunch.

"Kev, I've ridden that horse I told you of!" He paced about the room, too wound up to sit down. "He is everything I thought he'd be. Speed! You wouldn't believe how we flew!"

Kev eyed him complacently. "You're still flying. Sit down. I've only just eaten and you'll give me indigestion with your gyrations. I take it you've been to Deane Farm."

Tony threw himself into the one comfortable chair. "I was all wrong about Mrs. Deane. She is charming and not my enemy at all! If only I can convince her to let me ride in that race meet—it would be a triumph. And I mean to do it! She is a woman, after all."

Some of Kevin's complacency slipped. "I thought you considered her a veritable dragon."

Tony grinned and brushed a wayward lock of dark hair from his forehead. "That was while I believed her determined to keep me from Bella. Now she is all smiles when we meet." His eyes warmed reminiscently. "And such smiles. I declare, when she is not frowning at me, she is quite as beautiful as her sister. I have always preferred an older woman . . . and a widow!" He winked at Kevin and then suddenly shrank back in his chair. For some unaccountable reason, his brother had risen and stood over him, furious.

"Mind your tongue, you young idiot! Mrs. Deane is a lady and never forget it or you'll feel more than the back of my hand!"

Tony sat up, amazed. "Good God, Kev. I meant no harm. I thought you didn't like her!"

"I don't. She's a common, vulgar colonial and I want no connection with that family, do you understand? Now get out!"

Tony got slowly to his feet. "Make up your mind, old boy. You sound a bit confused. I begin to think you're more inclined that way than you know. No, don't mill me down! I'm going."

He went, but the knowing smile on his face left Kevin vaguely uneasy. He dismissed the feeling out of hand. Tony was a romantic young fool. His only feeling for that Deane vixen was one of admiration for her spirit.

But why this sudden friendliness to his brother after her loudly voiced opposition? What was her game? Had she decided to come out in the open and condone the affair between Tony and her sister since learning of his own fortune? That must be it. But why smile on Tony and not on him? Surely, he himself was the better prize. Must he now cut out his brother?

He caught himself up. Whatever was he thinking? He had no designs on that female! But he remembered her on the dancing horse, quite ravishing in a rose-colored habit, her golden curls escaping from her plumed hat as she easily controlled her mount. Yes, she came nigh to outshining her lovely sister.

Then he remembered another picture of Mrs. Deane, in filthy buckskins, her face white and terrified as she struggled to save Zephyr's foal. And white-faced again, this time with fury, grabbing up a bucket of water and deluging him. Tony could never appreciate her spirit. There was a woman worth taming, but his "Kate" would not be easily won. A foeman—or foewoman—worthy of his steel. The very Kate for his Petrucchio!

Good God, what had he just thought? His Kate! He

leaped to his feet, knocking over his chair. Was he out of his mind?

You're the fool, he told himself, picking up the chair. Wake up, man. Remember who she is! His first summation of her character must be correct. Anger, all out of proportion, cleared his head. She played brother against brother, she was after Tony for her sister all the time. If she wished to play out her little game, why he'd be glad to oblige. He'd soon break her to bridle. Whatever the result, he was in for no lasting affair. No filly, once he had tamed her, had ever held his interest. He always turned them over to someone else to ride.

When Charly and Bella returned to town, Aunt Augusta greeted them with delight, full of a scheme for their entertainment.

"The St. George's Society is sponsoring a charitable entertainment this evening at Corré's Mount Vernon Pleasure Garden, all out of doors, you know. There are to be acrobats, jugglers, singers, and comedians as well as a dramatic presentation. I believe it to be a most respectable affair, for Anabel Brougham told me of it, and she has volunteered to chaperon the both of you!"

Bella, who for some reason had been very silent on the drive to town, squealed with delight.

"It is not far, situated on Broad Way only a bit beyond the hospital," Augusta continued. "My coachman will take you all and bring you home. Everyone who is anyone will attend, I am sure. It will be a highlight of the Season!"

Charly caught an odd note in her voice and dropped to one knee beside the wheeled chair, hugging her aunt. "You are a dear, love. Oh, how I wish you would come too!"

"Well, now." Augusta patted her cheek. "Many is the time I've gone to the pleasure gardens and I've witnessed any number of fine presentations. Now run upstairs, both of you, and make ready."

She hesitated, picking at the afghan over her knees as Bella flew on her way. She glanced up at Charly, her firm expression failing to hide a guilty look in her eyes. Charly raised her eyebrows and waited.

"It is only that Jonathan Treadwell stopped by while Anabel was with me, and somehow he has become one of the party. No, now wait!" She raised a hand forestalling Charly's exclamation. "It is only right that you should have the protection of a gentleman in your party when you attend so public a function. I utterly forbade Anabel to venture to such a place on her own."

Charly smiled, thin-lipped. "It is quite all right, Aunt Augusta. I have a rather large bone to pick with Jonathan. As usual," she added.

Augusta's face fell. "Not more? I had hoped this evening would serve to patch up affairs between you two."

Charly stooped to kiss her puckered brow. "Give it up, love. There is no hope. However, I shall welcome a chance to settle at least one point tonight."

Unable to rake down Jonathan in a closed carriage, Charly had to contain herself and address him with cold politeness—when she spoke to him at all. Full of the evening's delights, he seemed unconscious of her frigid attitude. Thank goodness, she thought, she hadn't to put up with his thick-headed insensibility for the rest of her life. She would rather take up residence in the almshouse!

The first sight of Corré's Mount Vernon Pleasure Garden at night drew gasps of rapture from Bella. The outdoor park and theater sparkled in a fairyland of colored lights. Modeled after the famous Vauxhall gardens in London, it nearly outdid them. Lanterns were strung from the trees, where couples wandered along winding paths beyond the area in front of the stage were tables and boxes awaited the paying guests and waiters scurried about.

Jonathan secured them a place on the inner ring, where they could see everything and everyone. And be equally seen, Charly soon realized, for she caught Kevin Marlowe's eyes upon her as she sat down.

Bella had seen him, too, and more important to her, she saw his brother Tony beside him, and pointed them out to her sister. They were part of a large party, Charly noted with no little disapproval. A party made up of Mrs. Simone Galbraith's wide circle of rakish friends. He must feel right at home in such company, she thought, looking hastily away. How could the man manage to appear quite as magnificent in evening clothes as he did in riding gear on a horse? It seemed incongruous, both her ideals in one man. Physical ideals, she reminded herself, certainly not those of character.

It was all too depressing. If she was honest, which she had no desire to be, she found the man far too fatally attractive. But unattainable! It was his supercilious attitude toward her—and all of America—that hurt most deeply. Why must he be so socially ambitious? He was a successful man, wealthy by his own efforts; why could he not be content with the place that such attributes must surely win him here on this continent? Why must he return to his class-conscious England instead of discovering the pleasures of marriage with a kindred soul? Good heavens, an unwelcome admission! Was that what she truly wanted, what had been hiding in her mind while she thought of how much she disliked him? She felt her cheeks heat furiously and unfurled her fan to hide behind.

To add to her discomfiture, Marlowe looked up just then and caught her staring at him. For a brief moment, their eyes met across two tables and Charly experienced the oddest sensation, as if she almost forgot to breathe. Flustered, she looked away and said something at random to Miss Brougham.

"I beg pardon, my dear?" That lady turned to her, blinking in the lantern light. "I'm afraid I wasn't listening."

"Oh, nothing," Charly said, thankful she hadn't been heard since she couldn't remember what she had said. "I—I merely remarked that it is all very lovely."

As Miss Brougham went back to discussing the quizzes in the next box with Jonathan and searching the crowd for possible acquaintances, Charly became vividly aware that she faced complications. Anabel Brougham, for one, would enact her role of chaperon to both sisters with zeal. This put a real crimp in Charly's plan. Any attempt on her part to cast out lures to Tony would surely not pass unnoticed by Miss Brougham's sharp eyes. And there was Jonathan, not to mention Kevin Marlowe. No, she'd have to await a more propitious occasion.

Then she saw Tony watching their table. He nodded to her and she smiled invitingly. He came over to them at once, bowing gracefully to Miss Brougham before he took Charly's hand and raised her fingers to his lips.

"Mrs. Deane." A sparkling gleam lit his mischievous eyes. "Will you permit me to say that I have never seen you look so becoming?"

"Now how could I possibly object to such a lovely compliment?" In point of fact, she had taken great care with her appearance that night in case she should meet him, wearing a newly remodeled gown of Pomona green silk she had meant for Bella. Her need, she had decided, was greater. From the corner of her eye, she saw Kevin half rise, glowering. She played with her fan, demurely, as if overwhelmed by Tony's charm.

"You take the shine out of every other female present," he added, and she felt Bella stiffen by her side.

He only wanted to ride Summer Wind, she knew, but his admiration seemed sincere, and her plan took a firmer hold. Could she do it? She tried fluttering her eyelashes and was rewarded by a dazzling smile before he turned to her sister.

Bella's response was cold, and Charly eyed her anxiously. Letting Tony come to watch Wind, and even allowing him to ride the horse, was having a disturbing consequence. Bella obviously resented the way Tony now played up to her sister instead of herself, overlooking the fact that he only flattered Charly to get his own way. Bella was frankly annoyed, and Charly realized with some surprise that this must be the first time young Marlowe had devoted his charm to another female. Worse, Bella thought, Charly invited it. This was not at all what she had in mind. No, she must make it appear that Tony forced unwanted advances on her. And not here, in front of everyone. Somehow the act must be for Bella's edification alone.

Just then, Miss Brougham crowed happily and waved a ring-covered hand. Richard Cranford bore down on their table.

He bowed gallantly, favoring all with a friendly smile,

and requested permission to carry Miss Isabella off to see the colored lanterns in the walk behind them before the show began. Bella sprang up, all girlish delight, and accepted his arm. In a very few moments, her intentions became painfully obvious. When Richard Cranford smiled down at her, Bella responded with a fluttering of her fan and a coy look, and the two strolled off together. As they went, she cast a covert glance toward Tony, then immediately looked back at her companion.

Charly sighed. Bella was really very young. Tony must surely see through her attempts to make him jealous, but to her amazement, he bore every sign of being a victim of the green-eyed monster! He excused himself abruptly and went back to his own party.

Kevin Marlowe, she noted, seemed to be enjoying himself immensely, flirting with Mrs. Galbraith. Not that she cared, of course. She turned to Jonathan, who had risen angrily when Tony came up and still stood, looking remarkably like an annoyed stuffed frog.

"Come walk with me," she ordered. "If you will excuse us for a few moments, Miss Brougham. I have something to say to Jonathan."

Anabel Brougham beamed. Truly this evening proved all she could wish. Only wait until she could tell Augusta! Isabella strolling with Cranford, and now dear Charlotte going off with Treadwell! "By all means, my dear. I shall be quite all right here. Only hurry back; I do believe the orchestra is about to take its place."

"This will take only a minute," Charly assured her, grimly. She took Jonathan's arm and led him away. As soon as they were out of earshot, she began without preamble.

"There is something you and I must settle between us," she informed him in a tight undervoice.

"Certainly." A puzzled frown creased his brow as he followed her. As soon as they were clear of the crowd, she rounded on him.

"I understand you took it upon yourself to inform Mr. Van Bleek of my stallion's death."

Under the light of a green paper lantern his face took on a ghastly hue. His mouth opened but no words came out.

"How dare you talk about me—bandying my name again! And probably in such a public place as the Tontine Coffee House! Just how many were in your party this time? Am I to expect unwanted congratulations and offers for my property from every merchant in New York City?"

"No, no, really, you exaggerate, my dear!" Treadwell tried a conciliatory smile, apparently realized it did not go over well, and looked anxiously serious once more. "There were only the two of us. Knowing him to have an interest and being a friend of yours, I thought you would not take it amiss if I—"

"He is not a friend!" Charly stamped a foot. "Jonathan, if my name escapes your lips one more time, I shall . . . I shall . . ." Words failed her and she stalked back to the tables.

Refreshments had arrived while they were gone, no doubt ordered earlier by Treadwell. Lemonade and orgeat, impossibly thin slices of ham, tiny cucumber sandwiches, and plates of salmon mayonnaise which Charly abhorred. Just to be thoroughly contrary, suiting her mood, she selected a large dish of the salmon as the orchestra made tentative sounds and settled down.

The acrobats and jugglers did their best, and were appropriately applauded by all but Charly and Bella, both of whom seemed strangely abstracted. The first act of the dramatic performance gripped them even less. Had Charly not been so conscious of Mrs. Galbraith's lively party several tables away, she might have noticed Bella's frozen features.

The intermission brought Jonathan to his feet. He caught Charly's arm and tried to lead her away, but she pulled back.

"Let me go! Whatever are you about?"

"Please, Charlotte. Walk a bit with me; I must speak with you." He stood, blocking her view of the Galbraith table, and she looked past him to see Kevin Marlowe approaching.

Seeing Treadwell holding her by the arm, Marlowe stopped and shrugged, grinning at her before he made his way back to his party.

So that was what lay behind Jonathan's sudden need for exercise. He tried to keep her away from Kevin Marlowe! If she was not still so angry with him, she could almost be amused. If Kevin Marlowe sought her out, it would undoubtedly be with the intention of sparring with her.

To make matters worse, it dawned on her that Treadwell's obvious tatics merely entertained the irritating Mr. Marlowe. Being thwarted in his attempt to speak to her certainly hadn't upset him in the least. He had other amusement, quite certainly more suited to his libertine tastes. Before, Charly had been inclined to regard Mistress Simone Galbraith with tolerant contempt, but for some reason, she found her blatant flirtation with Kevin Marlowe this night disgusting and bordering on true vulgarity. If she did not know better, Charly might almost have believed herself to be suffering from jealousy. Somehow, she had come to consider the Marlowe brothers as the sole concern of herself and Bella.

Kevin seemed blissfully unaware, completely taken up with his new flirt while Charly was forced to put up with Jonathan. To her chagrin, she realized a real disappointment that he had been turned away, for his caustic and lively company was far more to her taste than Jonathan's constant effusive apologies. She tried again to pull her arm from his determined grasp.

"There now, my dear." Miss Brougham reached up and patted Charly's elbow. "Do go along with Jonathan, for I am about to carry Isabella off. I see the Andersons across the way, and I must make the child known to them, for they give the most delightful venetian breakfasts." She bustled to her feet. "I declare, I had no notion they were back in town. Augusta will be in ault. She is very fond of Beatrice Anderson."

She led an unprotesting Bella away, and Charly managed to free her arm and sit down.

"If you wish to please me, Jonathan, do not talk to me. See instead if you can procure some champagne punch or some wine, for I cannot bear orgeat."

Eager to make amends, he hurried off, and Charly sank back in her chair, closing her eyes.

"Oh, well done!" A deep, too familiar voice brought her sitting up straight and staring.

With all the charm of his younger brother and more, Kevin Marlowe took her limp hand, bowed low over it, and kissed her fingertips, the laughter in his eyes barely touching his lips.

Charly snatched back her hand. "Do you attend every social function in New York City, Mr. Marlowe?" she asked, pretending a disinterest she was far from feeling. "It seems we encounter you everywhere."

"After my somewhat disastrous encounters with you, I'm afraid I must, ma'am, if I intend to set foot out-of-doors at all. Almost my only undamaged garments consist of my evening wear." His eyes glinted with a suppressed merriment, inviting her to share the joke. "If I maintain my acquaintanceship with you, Mrs. Deane, I fear I may have to acquire an entirely new wardrobe." Without waiting to be asked, he took Jonathan's seat.

She raised haughty eyebrows at this impertinence, then quickly lowered her gaze as he turned his most devastating smile on her. At random, she picked up her plate of salmon mayonnaise and examined it closely.

"Your feelings seem to have changed regarding my brother," he said. "Unless I am much mistaken, it seems that you have several times made friendly overtures to him lately."

She straightened up in her chair, clutching the plate as if for support. "I see no reason to be impolite," she said coldly, but felt suddenly nervous.

"I suppose my brother's polished manners make a pleasant change from those of your boorish country swain."

Startled into defending Jonathan, she stood abruptly, still holding the salmon mayonnaise. "How dare you insult a man of such excellent . . . excellent . . . character!"

"Come, now," Kevin said, shaking his head. "Do not tell me you prefer the company of such a slowtop to mine." His disturbing smile flashed. "Sit down. Talk to me. You'll find me more entertaining than that cawker, I promise."

Secretly she agreed, but she was not about to give him the satisfaction of admitting it. His toplofty view of rustic Americans rankled.

"Or are you afraid?" he added in a provocative murmur. "Come, flirt with me, this is a night for pleasure."

Her cheeks burned. "I am no Simone Galbraith," she informed him in a tight whisper. The gleam in his eyes as he apparently considered the possibilities was too much for her. She spun away from him and the salmon mayonnaise, slippery at the best of times, spilled from her plate into his lap. Her hand at her mouth, she stifled a shriek of horror.

He stared down at the mess, and his shoulders began to quiver. "Madam"—he failed to control the laugh in his voice—"you have totally demolished me. As to its being purposely done this time, I give you benefit of doubt." He rose and bowed deeply, dripping salmon. "However, I fear I must retire from the lists."

Dismayed, she stared after him, unable to think of a single word to say. At least, she reflected suddenly, he could no longer dally with the Galbraith hussy.

Jonathan, who had been hovering in the background, strode up and handed her the glass of champagne. "I must congratulate you," he said. "You seem to have done an excellent job of sending that scoundrel to the rightabouts."

She had only moments to regain her composure, for Miss Brougham and Bella came right behind him. The orchestra had already picked up its instruments and the second act began. Charly found she had not the slightest idea of the plot, her mind having been elsewhere during the first performance. It did not seem to matter. She could not care less about the vicissitudes of the hapless heroine of the drama; she had enough troubles of her own. And why should the lady on the stage gain a happy ending when none was in sight for herself? Well, there was no time like the present for trying to resolve one unhappy situation.

The play drew to its predictable finale, and the stage was cleared for the inevitable musical numbers to follow. Charly got to her feet and turned to Miss Brougham. "Ma'am, do you mind if I walk about a bit? Just here behind us. I feel I must stretch after so long a sitting."

Jonathan jumped up. "I shall accompany you, Charlotte, you must not go alone!"

She fixed him with a quelling eye. "I *want* to be alone.

Now do remain here. I shall return before the entertainment ends.'' She pushed him back into his chair.

Miss Brougham looked at her anxiously. ''Do stay close, my dear. Within sight.''

Charly only smiled and walked off, passing close to the Galbraith table. Tony saw her, and she nodded invitingly. He winked, casually rose, and slowly followed her toward the lantern-lit trees.

Out of the corner of her eye, she caught Bella watching, an odd mixture of jealousy and puzzlement knitting her brow. Charly knew a momentary twinge of remorse at the pain she was about to cause her little sister if her plan worked, but it had to be done. Better this, by far, than allowing her to be either ruined or heartbroken over the Beautiful Tony. If he would just cooperate . . .

She stopped and turned back to him. ''Let us take the air,'' she suggested, sure that they were still in Bella's plain sight. ''The entertainment has become insufferably boring.''

He agreed with animation and offered his arm. She pretended to hesitate, then acquiesce. With care, she might manage to make it look to an observer as if the suggestion were his. She glanced back at Bella and saw her on her feet, her eyes on Tony as he led her sister away. Good. She would follow. She smiled up at Tony. ''I see your brother has deserted your party.''

''Has he?'' Tony didn't seem to care.

Charly giggled. ''He would still be there but for a little mishap involving my salmon mayonnaise.''

''Tell me!'' Tony demanded on the instant. ''Every detail!'' His eyes sparkled, and he laughed with real delight as she complied. ''Gets the old boy off my back. I cannot thank you enough.''

The story apparently broke down any last elements of reserve he might have felt. As they strolled beneath the trees, he flirted with her as outrageously as he did—perhaps unconsciously—with every pretty female. It seemed to be his natural style, and Charly worried for Bella. The girl took his advances too seriously.

More than ever before, Charly determined to break Bella of her infatuation. But while rescuing her sister, she must be careful. She had no desire to be compromised by the Beautiful Tony.

"Have you attended any races in America yet?" she asked. The ploy worked, and he answered eagerly.

"I have not. I cannot tell you how much I am looking forward to the meet at Maindenhead."

"It is a pity that Wind is so unpredictable." She sighed, very much the helpless female. "How do *you* go about handling a horse as high-spirited as Wind in his first race?"

He positively preened himself.

They were now beyond the sight of the tables. With so little difficulty that it left her nervous, she lured him along a path toward a gazebo. She barely glimpsed the glow of a cigar where someone blew a cloud inside it, and steered him away. "Do let us walk on." Playing with her fan as they went, she asked about racehorses he had ridden, pretending a fascination she did not really feel.

Apparently, this was all the invitation he seemed to need to indulge in a bit of elegant dalliance. Torn between keeping him at a proper distance and exposing him to Bella as the libertine he was, she glanced back over her shoulder. To her dismay, Bella had not followed them. She must not have been able to escape Miss Brougham's watchful eye. She wasted her time! Chagrined, Charly decided they had best return themselves. She had nothing to gain by this.

She turned to him, touching the hand that had just come to rest on hers. Too late, she realized he misinterpreted the gesture. There was a gleam in his eyes, and she began to fear she had gone too far—and knew it when he seized her by the shoulders and tried to kiss her. She struggled to get free and twisted her head so his lips landed on her ear.

Heavy footsteps pounded on the graveled path and they were abruptly pulled apart. One hand still gripping Charly's arm, Kevin Marlowe glowered at them both. He rounded on his brother.

"What the devil do you think you're at? You've damn well forgotten the manners due your breeding! But then," he added, scowling at Charly, "I know precisely whom to blame for this incident. Don't think I haven't seen the lures you've been casting out for my brother."

Charly stared at him, momentarily helpless and shaken. She had not expected the alacrity of Tony's cooperation in her scheme, but she could not have Kevin despising her.

"It . . . it is not what you think!" she said before she could stop herself. "It was all a plan. I wanted to show Bella what Tony is really like, that he doesn't care for her! That he'd flirt with anyone! I had no idea he would respond so . . . so violently!" She rallied, and defended herself. "I did not encourage him that much!" She glared at Tony, who stared at her with the oddest look of consternation in his eyes.

Kevin raised cold eyebrows. "What would you? He is a healthy young man, and you showed him a willing female. If you must play with fire, pick someone old enough to know the rules."

Before she realized what he was about, he dragged her into his arms and kissed her himself, thoroughly.

For a long moment, Charly was lost in a heaven of warmth and enveloping strength. The world receded, and she knew only the overwhelming sensation of coming home. This was right, this was all, and she responded with all the pent-up longing of her love-starved years.

He raised his head and stared down into her dazed face, his eyes widening in a sort of wonder. Then, releasing her abruptly, he grabbed Tony by the arm and the two walked off together, leaving her standing alone in the garden.

CHAPTER
Eleven

*N*ever, in all of her life, had Charlotte felt so mortified. Thank God that Bella had not followed her
after all! And what was she to do now? How could
she ever face either brother again? They must both think her
a complete and unprincipled fool! And worse, would Tony
tell Bella what she had tried to do? Oh, how he could twist
this tale to his advantage! Bella would never trust her again.

She sank onto a bench beneath the colored lanterns,
afraid to go back to the tables. What if the brothers spoke of
her behavior to anyone else? The scandal it would create!
And she'd had the effrontery to lecture Bella on propriety!

How many people had observed her leaving with Tony?
So preoccupied had she been with her ridiculous plan, so
anxious that Bella should note Tony's behavior, that she
hadn't thought to be circumspect. Had Anabel Brougham
seen her? An awful thought! There would not be a gossip in
all of New York City who would not have the story by
morning if that was the case!

As she sat there, chewing on the corner of her handkerchief, fighting back tears of humiliation, Jonathan Treadwell
came into sight. He peered from side to side down all the
branching paths as he approached, obviously looking for
her. There was nowhere to hide. She waited hopelessly to be
discovered.

"There you are!" he exclaimed, and there was only relief in his voice. "I knew you'd be alone."

She could either burst into tears or brave it out. The latter seemed the better course. "And what is that supposed to mean?" she asked, taking refuge in a casual tone.

"That Brougham female has an evil and suspicious mind," Treadwell informed her indignantly. "I told her you merely happened to pass that table and barely spoke to the Marlowe fellow."

So she had been seen by Anabel Brougham! At least she could count on Jonathan and his own gossiping to "correct" this story. For once, she ought to be glad of Treadwell's possessive attitude. He could be counted on to squelch any scandalous story concerning her, for his own sake!

"Come, my dear, the weather is turning quite chilly now. You should not be out here without your shawl." He took her hand and drew her to her feet. "Let us go back to the table and reassure Miss Brougham. She is, after all, acting as your chaperon tonight."

This last was said with an attempt at teasing humor that did not amuse Charly in the least. But in honesty, she had to admit that never had she been so glad to see Jonathan.

With a certain amount of trepidation, she entered the lighted area where the entertainment had just come to an end. To her dismay, Tony stood beside his table. He looked up as she walked by and his eyes widened as Treadwell followed closely behind. He looked startled—nervous—and hastily walked away without another glance at them.

Why, he must know of Jonathan's feelings for her! Charly realized. Treadwell had made it his business to see that everyone did. And from Tony's manner, he must think Treadwell might call him out! Almost, she could smile. Perhaps fear of retaliation from Treadwell would keep him silent. Oh, she had never expected to be so grateful for her unwelcome suitor!

Much to her relief, no comment was made in her hearing by anyone, even the redoubtable Miss Brougham. Charlotte knew she owed this reticence to her reappearance with Treadwell. They remained to watch the dancing that followed,

and Charly was thankful to see nothing more of either
Marlowe brother for the rest of the evening.

Her luck was not to last. The next morning, as she sat
alone eating an early breakfast before departing for the
farm, a message was brought up to her that Mr. Anthony
Marlowe had called and requested a word with her in
private. Sudden panic gripped her, leaving her ill with
apprehension. What did he mean to say? Would he have the
audacity to bargain with her for his silence? Trying not to
show her inward misgivings, she went down to him.

He stood with his back to the hall, staring out the
window, as she entered the drawing room. To her surprise, it
was a very chastened face that he turned toward her as her
trembling hand closed the door. He stepped forward, then
hesitated.

"Mrs. Deane," he began, looking every bit as cowed as
she had felt only a moment before. "There was no excuse
for my conduct, and I most humbly beg your pardon. I can
only plead a combination of your loveliness, an excess of
champagne punch..." He shook his head. "I fear all added
together caused me to act in a manner unbefitting a gentleman. I simply lost my head. I pray you will forgive me."

"Of... of course," Charlotte stammered in her relief. He
made no mention of her confession that she had led him on
intentionally! In fact, he took the blame completely upon
himself. Here was chivalry she had not expected to encounter in such a heedless young gentleman.

"My brother raked me over the coals pretty thoroughly
last night," he added, his boyish smile flashing now that the
worst of his confessional ordeal was over. Suddenly he
sobered. "But if you wouldn't mind..." He broke off,
embarrassed once more.

"Yes?" She held her breath, waiting for his ultimatum.

"Please, don't tell Bella," he begged in a rush. "I meant
no harm."

"You may be sure I will not!" So the incident was to be
forgotten, as simply as that. Yet there was something that
still disturbed her, an unspoken apology in his manner that
she could not quite place, for it seemed to have nothing to

do with the unpleasant scene of the night before. Could it be for giving her the need to protect her sister in such a way, in the first place?

She took advantage of his chastened mood. "May I hope, sir, that you will now be more circumspect in your treatment of Bella?"

"Of that you may be sure." He held out his hand and she took it with an involuntary smile. Tony could be a charming rascal, particularly in this repentant mood.

She walked out into the hall with him, then turned him over to Jensen, who showed him to the door. As she started toward the stairs, Bella popped out of the cupboard beneath them, her lovely face flushed and eager.

"Did he . . . what did he wish to speak to you about?" she demanded. "Oh, please, Charly, tell me at once!"

Charlotte stared at her sister in dismay. Good God, she must believe Tony had come to ask for her hand! She braced herself for the inevitable. "Why, nothing to be so excited about, Bella." She kept her tone light and airy as she told her white lie. "He only came to beg once more to ride Wind in the race."

Bella stared at her. "He . . . he came about riding Wind?" she repeated.

"Of course, you silly goose. What else would he want so desperately?" Charly forced a casual laugh. "And now, I wish to finish my breakfast. Are you coming?"

Her heart sank at sight of Bella's face. The affair must have gone even further than she had feared. The girl was truly in love. Charly could only count on Tony's promise to behave with propriety and allow his interest in Bella to appear to wane.

Bella, however, took matters into her own hands. Arriving at a soiree in the company of their Aunt Augusta, Charly and Bella almost collided with Tony the moment they entered the drawing room. Bella stopped dead, color flooding her cheeks, and she turned abruptly on her heel and walked away, snubbing him in no uncertain manner. In another moment, she had joined Richard Cranford, who greeted her with a warm smile.

"Now, that is a pleasant sight," Aunt Augusta declared,

as Charly pushed in the wheeled chair that had been carried up the stairs by the two footmen. "If only the chit will accept Cranford and you would marry Treadwell, I could die happy."

"You are not going to die for many years yet." Charly patted her shoulder. "Bella and I will meet a lot of other men before you are gone."

Bella's treatment of Tony did not please Charly as much as it might, for she knew that it sprang from chagrin rather than indifference. Nor was her mood lightened by the presence of Kevin Marlowe. To her mixed relief and dismay, he made no move to come near her. Instead, she had the dubious pleasure of watching him across the room, flirting again with Simone Galbraith.

Did he kiss his scandalous *chère amie* the way he had kissed her? Charly wondered. Simone Galbraith might be more willing, but the effect on that lady could hardly be more stunning. Giving her head a shake to clear her thoughts, Charly went to seek out refreshments for her aunt.

Her lingering fears about the night before began to dissipate. Kevin, as well as Tony, seemed to be keeping quiet about her reprehensible behavior, and no one else must have seen her walk off with Tony. No whispers did she catch as she passed, no snubs did she receive from the high sticklers. Her name, thankfully, appeared free from sordid gossip. She had been lucky beyond her desserts for trying such a scatterbrained stunt.

As she returned carrying two glasses of ratafia, she glanced at Kevin, who stood in very close proximity to Mrs. Galbraith. Indecently so, Charly thought. At that inopportune moment, he chose to look up and met her gaze across the room. A crease formed in his brow as his eyes rested on her. He started to excuse himself, but Mrs. Galbraith laid her hand on his arm and whispered something in his ear. He turned his full attention back to his companion. In a very few minutes, they walked out of the room together and did not return again that evening. For some inscrutable reason, Charly had trouble sleeping that night.

Still restless the next morning, she called for her light chaise and drove old Bruno out to the farm to see her colt.

He was growing fast, but he was light-boned, just as Kevin Marlowe had predicted.

Why did everything have to bring that man to mind? Let him flirt with that far too free Galbraith female! She didn't care! Her only objection to that shameless connection was that it would likely keep him in New York, while she longed for him to leave—and take the Beautiful Tony with him!

She frowned as she studied the colt running in the pasture. Were his light bones his only fault? Summer Wind had inherited their sire's disposition and was frequently almost impossible to control. Would this colt have it, too? She watched, anxious, for any signs of this to manifest, but it was hard to tell in one so young. At the moment, he was solely concerned with nursing and play.

The breeze, which had lightly ruffled her hair on the drive out, now blew in heavy gusts. It bade fair to be a windy day. She clutched her shawl about her, and turning from the pasture, she made her way to the lane and leaned on the fence while Ben Stokes exercised Summer Wind on the flat roadway. The horse was playing off his tricks, nervous amid the swirls of dust and flying leaves, looking for any excuse to shy and prance. Wild weather always upset him, but so far, Ben seemed to have him easily under control.

Then as Ben started him down the straightaway once more, a rabbit sprang from the underbrush by the lane, right under Wind's nose. The horse reared and plunged, and chaos reined for the next few seconds. As Charly watched, horrified, the saddle girth gave way. Ben was thrown hard, the horse bolted, and Charly screamed. She started to scramble over the rail fence, hampered by her long skirts. Poised at the top, she stared down the lane where the horse had already vanished. Running footsteps came up behind her and she turned.

"Jim! Get another horse and go after Wind!" she called. "And Henry! Come help me with Ben!"

She climbed down into the lane and ran to the side of the fallen man.

"My . . . my shoulder," Ben gasped. He tried to rise and sank back down on the ground. "I think it's broken."

"Henry, take one of the mares and ride for the doctor!"

Charly commanded. She went down onto her knees. "Lie back, Ben, don't try to move." Pulling off her shawl, she rolled it into a pad for his head.

"Now I've done it," he whispered through gritted teeth. "Landed us in the suds right proper, I have, Mrs. Deane."

Charly stared down at him as the meaning of his words dawned on her. He would not be able to ride Wind at the race meet. Now what was she to do? It seemed awful to worry about herself with Ben like this, but their future—that of all of them—rested on the outcome of this race. If Wind did not win...if the worth of her bloodline was not proved...She saw the price of her yearlings dropping, the mortgage on the farm not being met. She felt the blood drain from her cheeks until she was as pale as Ben.

She sat in the dirt beside him, waiting. Ben had closed his eyes and seemed asleep except for a muscle twitching in one leather cheek. The only sign of the agony he must be feeling showed in his tight lips and the white line about his mouth.

It seemed ages before Henry returned, cantering behind the doctor's ancient gig, though it probably was less than an hour. Dr. Crofton, a kindly man who had seen Bella and both farm boys through the measles a few years before, greeted Charly with a grunt and knelt beside Ben. He ran light hands over the shoulder, grunting again, but with reassurance, when his patient winced.

Ben managed a few words. "Broke it, did I?"

The doctor sat back, "What, an old whipstock like you? Bend double, you would, before you broke. It's just pulled out of the socket, dislocated. You'll be right as rain in six...seven weeks."

Six weeks! The race meet was less than two weeks away.

Dr. Crofton, helping Ben to sit up, failed to see the stricken look in Charly's eyes. "Henry, there's a roll of linen strapping on the buggy seat, get it like a good lad. We'll have to wrap the arm against his chest before we move him. Any more injuries, Ben?" He felt both legs and gently tapped Ben's ribs. "Not to worry, Mrs. Deane. No other damage that I can see."

None that could be seen! Only the crashing about her

head of all her hopes and plans. Ben would not possibly be able to ride Wind in time for the race.

Henry had brought the roll of linen, and she watched Dr. Crofton secure the arm so Ben could move with the least pain. The two men got him to his feet and supported him down the drive to his cottage. Charly held the door as they helped him inside and laid him on the bed.

Jim stuck his head into the doorway. "I caught Wind, ma'am. He's all right. I put him in his stall and I carried in the broken saddle." He licked his dry lips, looking over at Ben, lying white-faced on the bed. "Is . . . is he going to die?"

Dr. Crofton laughed. "No such luck, Jim lad. Stay here, I can use you. Mrs. Deane, you and Henry get out. Go up to the house and bring me some brandy. We'll have to re-settle that shoulder joint before it gets any more inflamed."

Silas Hawkes, sitting on one of his Morgans, rode up to Charly and Henry as they came out the door. "Just saw Jim," he called down. 'How's old Ben?'

Charly stopped. "Henry, go and ask Myra for the brandy. Tell her it's in the corner cupboard." She turned back to Silas. "It's not too bad. He's just dislocated his shoulder . . . but he won't be able to ride, not for weeks and weeks."

Silas had no need to be told what that meant.

"That's a bad turn for you, Mrs. Deane." He rubbed his chin. "Mighty bad, what with you counting on that race meet and all." Reaching down, he touched a comforting hand to her cheek and went on, gruffly. "You just remember my offer, and don't you worry none. I'll give you a price that'll be more than fair."

She looked up at him, two bright spots of color burning in her cheeks. "I'm not going to give in! I won't! I'll find another rider."

Appreciation, diluted with pity, softened his eyes. He half-shook his head. "Good luck to you, girl."

He turned his horse and cantered off, leaving Charly feeling sick with worry. And out of her despair came a picture of Tony Marlowe riding Wind down that same lane. Tony could ride Wind. She was over a barrel. What could she do but ask him to take over for Ben? Bella said he raced in Ireland. He said he always won. But could he handle Wind?

She had no choice. The only sensible thing might be to give up and cancel the race, but too much depended on its outcome. She'd have to take the only chance she had. She'd have to eat humble pie and ask Tony Marlowe to ride for her—after the humiliating scene she'd enacted at the pleasure garden.

CHAPTER

Twelve

*H*enry had not returned with the brandy, and Charly hurried toward the house after him. She almost collided with Myra, who came running frantically around the corner of the barn carrying the decanter.

Charly caught her and tried to take the decanter, but Myra's desperate fingers clutched it like a lifeline. "Ben's all right, Myra," she cried. "Dr. Crofton says he's not seriously injured."

Myra blinked, and recovered her usual poise and caustic tongue. "I knew the fool would break his neck one of these days." She surreptitiously wiped at one cheek. "No sense is what he has. No sense at all."

"Not his neck." Taking her hand, Charly made haste toward the cottage. "Or any bones broken. He's only dislocated his shoulder."

Myra sniffed. "Sooner we're rid of these crazy horses the better for all of us."

Charly could not let this pass. "It was the saddle girth. It broke just as Wind lunged."

Dr. Crofton forestalled Myra's tart answer, meeting them at the door as Henry came panting up behind. He pried the decanter from Myra's deathlike grip and peered at her closely.

"Take her back to the house, Mrs. Deane. I have no need

of two hysterical females. I prescribe a large glass of your best wine for each of you and keep out of my way. Won't take but a few minutes once the brandy takes hold. I'll send Jim up for you when I'm done."

There seemed nothing to do but obey his orders. Myra already had begun to tremble from reaction, and Charly steered her back to the main house, where she poured a generous glass for each of them.

They sat on the piazza, waiting. Myra straightened her apron, patted at her mob cap, and finally, with an embarrassed throat clearing, spoke.

"I beg pardon, Mrs. Deane, for acting such a ninny, but I've never left off expecting to find him killed by one of those horses."

Charly managed a smile. "You should have seen me go over the fence when it happened." She glanced down ruefully. "I forgot I wasn't wearing my buckskins and this skirt will never recover, although Ben will."

The atmosphere lightened, but not Charly's heart. Deane Farm had little chance of recovery either.

When Jim appeared at last, they walked back to the cottage, where Dr. Crofton had finished putting the shoulder back in place. He addressed Myra cheerfully.

"Rest and quiet is all he needs now for a day or so. I've given him a draft that should keep him asleep until tomorrow. Have you any laudanum to hand?" He continued briskly as Myra nodded. "Good. Give him a few drops in water to ease the pain if he seems to be suffering. It should settle down in a few days." He turned to Charly. "But no work with the horses for at least a month. You've got Jim here, he's a good handy lad and he can take over."

Young Jim swelled with pride and seemed to grow a few inches taller as the doctor bade them all farewell and climbed back into his gig.

Myra went in to sit with Ben after Dr. Crofton's departure, and Charly conferred with her new farm manager. He was eager to review the plans to guard the farm at night, and Charly listlessly agreed to his suggestions. Secretly, she felt that nothing mattered anymore. Once her unknown foe learned of Ben's injury, he might well be satisfied, for unless, by some miracle, Wind would win his races without Ben in the saddle, she was as good as ruined.

Surprised to find it was still early in the day, she had Henry hitch Bruno to her chaise. Jim was now above such menial tasks. She drove slowly back to Beaver Street, working up her courage to face Tony Marlowe after flatly refusing to let him ride in the meet and quite clearly letting him know she didn't think him rider enough. He would have every right to take a pique and turn her down. She had never been his friend.

She found Bella in a strange mood. When Charly poured out the story of Ben's accident and finished with her plan to ask Tony to ride Wind, Bella stiffened and adopted a studiously indifferent attitude.

"But do you think Tony can do it?" Charly asked anxiously.

Bella tossed her head. "Certainly Mr. Marlowe claims he can ride. How can I know if he spoke the truth?" She busied herself packing up the needlework she had been doing, hiding her expression. "I couldn't care less what he does. If you are sure Ben will not recover in time, why, you must do as you see fit."

Augusta twisted her kerchief in her gnarled hands. "Jim?" she asked, but Charly shook her head.

"He hasn't the experience. He's never been in a race nor has he sat on Wind more than two or three times, and then just to walk him."

"More than Tony has done," Bella muttered.

Exasperated, Charly sighed. Bella's disappointment over Tony's visit had been bitter. Well, maybe now her ardor would cool. How odd that now, when there was a chance of the affair coming to an end, she had to bring Tony back into constant contact.

For once, they had no evening engagement. She sat down at her aunt's writing desk and composed a carefully worded message to Tony, asking him to call on her at his earliest convenience, and dispatched it via Augusta's coachman.

He arrived less than half an hour later, but he was not alone. His brother Kevin came with him. It was the first time Charly had actually spoken to him since the debacle by the gazebo, and she shrank inside, but he greeted her as though it had never happened. Bracing herself, she told them what had occurred.

Kevin's brow snapped down and Tony looked suitably sympathetic—until his eyes opened wide as he realized the probable meaning of her summons.

"Do you mean *I* may ride Wind in the race?" he demanded, his eyes sparkling.

"I'm afraid I have no other choice."

Kevin snorted. "Prettily said, Mrs. Deane," he remarked and Charly flushed.

"The race is too important for me to rely on anyone other than Ben. You certainly know that. But as your brother has kindly offered—"

"And it will be a pleasure to assist you!" Tony interrupted. "I shall have to ride him every day, to get the feel of him," he went on, pacing the room in his excitement. "I will go out to the farm first thing in the morning . . . that is, with your permission, Mrs. Deane? . . . and talk to your man, find out everything I can, and then—"

"Yes, you may spare us a recital of your plans," Kevin broke in.

Jensen arrived just then with refreshments Charly did not remember ordering, and she thanked the excellent butler. The gentlemen each accepted a glass of Augusta's best sherry.

"To the race!" Tony cried, raising his glass.

Charly joined in the toast, nearly choking in her relief.

Tony dropped into a chair, a dreamy smile on his face, lost in plans and dreams, and Kevin drew Charly down on the sofa beside him. "You really have all your hopes placed on this race," he said matter-of-factly.

"Yes." Her voice sounded somewhat hollow, and he gave her a crooked smile.

"Tony really is an excellent rider," he assured her. He hesitated, then added, "Though I fear your Summer Wind may not be up to his weight. He rides all of twelve stone."

Charly studied her clasped hands. "It seems I have no choice. I may either let Tony ride, or go and visit Mr. Van Bleek right now."

"No, not you!" Kevin declared, with surprising firmness.

"No," Charly agreed. "I am not one to give up without a fight, you may be sure."

"I had noted that," Kevin said, a smile in his voice.

She looked up into his face and felt an odd response quiver within her, warmed by his sympathy—and his surprising concern. It was almost as if he cared what happened to her! But he had recommended the extension. He probably didn't want to be proven wrong. After all, he had his reputation to think of! But she did not totally discount his concern, and she was grateful.

He stood, and she found herself rising with him, still gazing up into the gently understanding eyes that held hers. He raised her fingers to his lips.

"We will take our leave of you now. And do not worry. Tony will do his best for you. We both will." Rousing his brother from his reverie, he steered him out the door, leaving Charly to wonder about his last words—and about the odd warmth of his attitude. Sympathy for a fellow horse lover about to lose her precious animals? That was probably all it was, though that thought did not make her happy.

She dropped back onto the sofa, staring blindly out the window.

Barely minutes later, Jensen announced the arrival of Jonathan Treadwell, who came quickly into the room without waiting for her assent that she would receive a visitor.

"I just saw those Marlowe brothers riding down the street!" he began, his tone almost accusing. "Had they the affrontery to bother you?"

"No," she responded coolly. "I sent for Mr. Anthony Marlowe."

Treadwell puffed out his cheeks. "What the devil!" With difficulty, he regained control of himself. "I beg pardon. What did you want with him?"

Charly steadied her voice. She might as well tell him now as later. "Ben has been injured, which left me without a rider for the race meet. Mr. Marlowe is quite experienced, and he had already offered to ride for me."

"Good God, surely you don't trust that ramshackle fellow!" In spite of his words, Treadwell seemed to be secretly pleased. He sat on the sofa beside her and reached for her hands. She withdrew them, instead picking up her glass of barely touched wine.

"Will you not join me in a glass of sherry? We have been toasting my chances at the meet."

"For heaven's sake, give it up, Charlotte! You have been defeated! And by circumstances beyond your control. That is no disgrace! You must sell the farm while you can still demand a high price, and marry me."

Charly set her glass on the table with a force that made the wine splash on the polished wood. She mopped at it hastily with her handkerchief. "I am not defeated until my last chance has failed! And I will never stop fighting."

Jonathan frowned. "You know I have always admired your spirit, Charlotte," he pronounced, quite untruthfully. "But there comes a time when good sense must prevail. You have nothing to gain and a very great deal to lose if your horse does not win this race—for whatever reason. Would it not be better to have that precious bloodline of yours untried rather than proven inferior?"

This she did not need. She stood, angry. "Inferior, is it? That is something we shall not know until after the race, is it not?" She jerked on the bell pull with unnecessary force, bringing Jensen almost at the run. "Good day, Mr. Treadwell," she spoke in frozen accents, and once more Jonathan departed, wallowing in apologies.

Charly's knees gave out, dropping her back onto the sofa. How dare Treadwell strike out at her when she was down, knocking away what precious little confidence remained to her! Even Kevin Marlowe had been encouraging when he might have made some snide remark!

The following morning, Bella announced casually that she had no desire to accompany her sister to the farm. She had other things to do, plans to walk in City Hall Park with her friends. At least she can't be meeting Tony, Charly reflected, though she was not overly pleased. Bella's eyes glinted in an unsettling way. That her plan was some way to bring Tony up to scratch, Charly could not doubt. The question that gave her pause was *how*?

When she reached the farm, Tony was there before her. He came out to meet the carriage—and his face fell as he saw her alone.

"Bella does not come to see me ride?" he called as she drew up.

"Not today at any rate." Charly settled the whip into its socket. "She claims previous plans."

Tony seemed puzzled. "I fancied her manner a bit odd when last I saw her." His face paled as a horrid thought struck him. "You . . . you did not tell her!"

"Of course not! Do you think me a ninny? Besides, the . . . the fault was mine. I'll be forever grateful if you will forget the incident ever happened."

He grinned. "Oh, I have, truly, as much as old Kev will let me. I say," he scrubbed a toe in the dirt, "I've been in to speak with your man. He did not know I was to ride, and I don't believe the news sat well with him. However"—Tony's delighted boyish grin returned—"I told him it was either me or young Jim and he said, given a choice, he'd rather it was I who would be killed."

"That sounds like Ben." Insensibly cheered by this sign of a resurgence of Ben's spirits, she accepted Tony's hand and allowed him to help her down from the chaise. Henry had come running up, full of his new importance as he took over one of Jim's duties, and she handed him the reins. Tony paced beside her, shortening his long strides as they walked to Ben's cottage.

"He says I am not to get on Wind yet. He has a great deal to tell me about the horse's idiosyncrasies first."

Charly nodded. "Best do as he says. No one knows that . . . that unpredictable horse as well as Ben does." It sounded as though Ben had accepted the inevitable. Thank goodness, she thought, one less difficult male to deal with. Now why should she feel an odd regret that Kevin had not accompanied Tony?

"Your brother and my sister are both leaving us to our own devices. Is he not interested in watching you either?"

"Oh, Kev is off on some business of his own this morning. But he wished our enterprise good luck before he left." And with that, Charly had to be satisfied.

Tony spent the morning receiving a detailed lecture on Summer Wind. Ben, his arm strapped to his side and his weathered face drawn with pain, took the young man over and over the fine points of dealing with a high-couraged, incorrigible mount. Not until he finally admitted that Tony had his lessons down word perfect, did he allow Tony to visit the horse.

Though excited, Tony confined himself to watching how Wind moved in the pasture and then lunging him, seeking out his strengths and weaknesses.

"Kev never allowed me to do this part of the training," he confided with a blissful smile. "I've often watched him to pick up a few pointers, but I never understood what he was doing until now. That Ben of yours is a true master!"

For the first time, Charly saw a serious, capable side to the Beautiful Tony. He won her grudging respect—in regard to handling horses at least.

The next few days passed in long hours of work with Wind. Charly and Tony spent every day at the farm, though Charly had to be back in town by late afternoon to prepare for the evening round of parties Bella insisted on attending. Ben could now stand by, coaching Tony, and Charly was surprised again at how tenacious Tony could be when engrossed in a project he cared about, racing to win. So concerned was she in preparing Wind and Tony for the race meet that she had almost forgotten the earlier attempts to ruin her. Jim and Henry reported that all was quiet at the farm at night, but they assured her they were not letting up on their vigilance—if that was what their enemy hoped for.

Bella, still hurt, shunned the training sessions, pretending an indifference Charly knew she was far from feeling. But Charly could give her no hope of any sort, for Tony said nothing more to her about Bella's defection. It was possible he really did not care and, spoiled boy that he was, the horse and the race were now all consuming to him.

At an evening party four days later, Charly suddenly came out of her own abstraction to become aware that Bella flirted almost desperately with Cranford, leading him on, although she still did not want to accept his offer, despite

Aunt Augusta's urgings. Vexed with herself for being so involved in her own problems, Charly began to worry about Bella again. She acted too happy, laughed too quickly, and chattered too much. There was a bright color in her cheeks, but misery in her eyes when she looked away.

She'll have to wait, Charly told herself. I haven't time for her now. First the race, then I'll cope with Bella.

She stayed at the farm that night, for the meet was only three days away, and she was to meet Tony very early the next morning. As she extinguished her candle and plunged her room into darkness, she caught a glimpse of a bobbing light in the back pasture.

Dragging on a dressing gown and a pair of boots, she ran down to awaken Jim and Henry. Outside the barn, she ran into Ben, his white bandaged shoulder gleaming in the faint moonlight. "Ben?"

"Yep, I saw it, too," he whispered, although there was no chance of their voices carrying so far. Silently they felt their way along the paddocks and out into the field. The light remained, never still, yet in the same place.

"Why doesn't he stop and run?" Charly wondered. "We must be in plain sight by now, even in the dark!"

"Because he's not there." Ben spoke aloud. "Look!" They reached the fence, and a lantern hung from the top rail, swinging in the wind so that it looked as though it was carried in someone's hand. The fence had not been touched.

"Why?" Charly asked. "Is this a joke?"

Ben had already untied the lantern and now he started back across the field at an ungainly run. "To lure us out here," he yelled. "Got to get back!"

Terror for her horses lending wings to her feet, Charly caught up and passed him. At the paddocks, she met Jim, carrying Ben's musket.

"Someone ran through here, ma'am. I didn't see who, but it was a man. Maybe the same one, because he had a horse in the lane like before! The horses are all right. I checked the stalls when I knew I couldn't catch the thief."

Ben was leaning over something in the corner of Wind's paddock. "Mrs. Deane, look here! A pile of moldy hay. You can lay odds none of us put that there."

Charly and Jim both came over, Jim bending down to sniff the hay. He wrinkled his nose. "Wind would never touch that stuff. The smell is enough to put off even the hungriest horse."

Charly clung to the paddock rails. "Someone tried to kill Wind?"

"Well," Ben considered the hay pile judiciously. "Mebbe not kill him but it would have made him awful sick." He glanced at her white face. "Put him right out of the race, that would."

Charly sat down hard on the edge of the water trough. This was a definite attempt to keep Wind out of the meet. She watched the men gather every last moldy straw from the ground. Ben held the lantern close to make sure they got it all.

"We'd best burn it in the morning, Jim. You and Henry see to it."

"Yes, sir!" Jim forked the pile into a barrow. "I'll lock this in the barn for tonight so's no one can get at it."

Kevin Marlowe rode out with Tony the next morning as Charly, Ben, and the two boys stood around the bonfire in a corner of the stable yard.

"A funeral pyre?" the irrepressible Tony asked. "You all look so serious."

"Another attempt." Charly turned to Kevin. "Has Tony told you of our problems?" In a few carefully chosen words, she repeated the tale of the bullet behind Summer Storm's ear, the night prowler who had led to his own fall into the puddle, the rusty nails, and now the lantern and moldy hay.

He looked at her curiously. "Doesn't an odd circumstance in all this occur to you?"

"What do you mean?"

"Why, that your villain is singularly inept. He shoots your horse at a range where he could not fail to kill. He falls over buckets in the dark. And now this. I would say it was someone who doesn't know much about horses. Damn few nags as well fed as yours would set a lip to moldy hay."

Charly stared at him. "A city man. Not Silas Hawkes, for sure."

"Do you mean your neighbor? Tony tells me he seems an honest, decent man. He even offered a few pointers the other day when he stopped to watch Tony ride."

"Yes." A burden seemed to be lifted from Charly's shoulders. She was fond of Silas, and it had really pained her to include him among her suspects. But there were others in the field. Van Bleek or one of his hired minions; Bentley; even Jonathan, though she was sure he hadn't the nerve or the inventiveness. The other horse breeders could now be eliminated also. Unless, of course—suppose these clumsy attempts were meant to distract her from the neatness of Storm's demise?

The fire had burned out and Tony came by leading Wind, saddled and ready to go, with Jim by his side. Ben signaled to Henry to dump the bucket of water that stood nearby over the last embers, and went to join Tony. Charly and Kevin followed, stopping at the front fence to lean on the top rail and watch Tony put the horse through his paces.

So far, Kevin had made no mention of her idiotic performance at the pleasure garden, and now Charly brought up the subject herself, determined to clear the air for she found it impossible to ignore.

"Your brother claims to care for my sister. If so, why did he so easily follow my lures and make love to me at the pleasure garden?"

"I'm afraid Tony has been spoiled from infancy. He soon learned he could get anything he wanted by using his physical beauty. He wished to ride your horse at Maidenhead. It would naturally occur to him that to exploit your apparent infatuation with his appearance would be the way to reach his goal."

"And that is the man my foolish little sister has set her heart on."

"Has she?" Kevin frowned. "It is most unwise of her."

"When is youth ever wise?" Charly demanded.

"It won't do," Kevin echoed an earlier conversation. "But do not think he has mercenary aims in mind. He would not marry her to gain possession of Deane Farm, even if it were solvent, I assure you. He knows I would buy him land in England or Ireland to establish his own estate as soon as he is creditably married.''

"I dismissed that idea some time ago," she informed him. "What I fear most is that his intentions are not marriage. And Bella, sweet innocent that she is, would never believe it."

Kevin shook his head. "For the life of me, I cannot see the attraction such a green female as your sister could hold for him."

"Oh, can you not?" She rounded on him, flying to the defense of her beloved sister. "Bella is a beauty and as sweet in disposition as she is lovely in face! Any man would glory in the possession of such a wife!"

"Or mistress?" he asked gently.

Charly shuddered. Looking up into Kevin's face, she felt every bit as young and vulnerable as Bella. The Marlowe charm was as unconscious as it was overwhelming. He grinned suddenly, causing her traitorous heart to skip a beat.

"He is not all bad, you know. His only sin is in capitalizing on his good looks, and he never uses that to cause pain or discomfort to any female. Witness his refusal to marry for position."

"I am witnessing his callow treatment of my sister! Does he not realize what he has done to her innocent heart?"

Marlowe frowned again. "I am afraid he may fancy himself in love, for there is never a vicious or mean thought in his mind. He is wholeheartedly kind and generous." A wry smile quirked up the corners of his mouth in a fascinating manner. "Unlike you, I fear his intention may well be matrimony. Your sister could do far worse . . . and he," he added firmly, "can do far better, for she is naught but a shallow little widgeon. Do not worry, as long as I hold the purse strings, he will not marry her."

Charly, unable to decide if she should be glad or furious, turned her back on him, concentrating on the sight of Tony flying past them along the quarter-mile dirt road.

The rout that evening turned into an informal dance. Kevin Marlowe found it rather enjoyable, for not only was Simone Galbraith present and teasingly inviting, but Mrs.

Charlotte Deane was positively looking arrows at her. A thoroughly delightful situation, and one that brought on a completely unexpected sense of elation. He pushed it down firmly, reminding himself that he only toyed with the Deane woman. She was a challenge, that was all, and he never could resist the chase of an elusive quarry.

Suddenly he became aware of another challenge from an unforeseen quarter. Young Miss Isabella had changed her tactics and now had eyes only for Tony once more. This he could not like, but its result brought him up short. Cranford looked puzzled at Bella's desertion, but instead of trying to lure the girl back, he had turned to her sister.

While Kevin watched, his annoyance taking fantastic leaps, Cranford stood up twice with Charlotte. And she seemed to be vastly enjoying his company! His irritation grew. Cranford was a man of the world, just the person to coax Isabella away from Tony; why must he dance with Charlotte and the two of them have such a good time? Disgruntled, Kevin turned back to Simone, but for some reason her sensuous caresses held no charm. What a man really needed was the open, honest response of a woman who kissed a man because she wanted him, wholeheartedly for all time, not for momentary sexual excitement. A woman who responded to a man the way . . . the colored lanterns of the pleasure garden danced before his mind's eye; a soft, fragrant form filled his arms; and warm lips met his, honestly, openly, with no coy artifice. Good God, this would never do!

On her part, Charly found Bella's sudden change equally upsetting. Apparently she had decided that making Tony jealous would not do the trick and she now had come out in the open in her pursuit. And Tony welcomed her back. But what of poor Richard Cranford? Charly sincerely hoped that Bella had done his heart no irreparable damage. None, at least, that could not be healed. He stood by himself on the edge of the dance floor. Simone Galbraith was thoroughly occupied casting out her lures to Kevin Marlowe—the hussy! Overcome with guilt for Bella's actions, Charly turned her attention to cheering Richard Cranford. She enjoyed considerable success and passed quite a pleasant evening, not a little of it due to the obvious dudgeon of Jonathan Treadwell.

In the morning, Tony arrived at the farm in a borrowed gig rather than on horseback as he usually came. Her heart sank as she saw the reason. Bella sat beside him. As she watched from her parlor window, Tony drew the carriage to a halt beneath the huge elm tree in the lane and turned to his companion. Bella raised her face and he touched a hand to her cheek. Their lips met for a long moment, then he picked up the reins and drove through the gate, unaware that they had been observed.

Charly greeted them as they handed over the equipage to Henry and got out. Bella's cheeks were flushed, and Tony could only be said to look smug.

"Well, Bella?" Charly began.

Her sister made a great play of settling her skirts. "I thought I'd come and watch today. After all, it is the last time before the race."

Charly waited, but no announcement of a betrothal came. Tony ran off to find Jim and saddle Wind. Bella talked airily of the party the night before and turned almost immediately to the coming race meet and Tony's undoubted prowess.

"Everything will come right, Charly. Only wait and see." She bubbled with repressed excitement, and Charly knew a real fear for her little sister. Bella quite certainly believed she had won, but an honorable man did not kiss girls secretly in the lane unless his intentions were honest. Tony should have come to her at once, as Bella's guardian, and asked her permission for their marriage. Not only did he not do so, he now casually carried on as if nothing had happened.

But the meet was on the morrow. She could not cope with Tony and Bella now. Her mind was too preoccupied to be rational. After the race, after all was well with her farm, she'd take Bella aside and tell her a few home truths.

Tony went back to town, but Bella elected to spend the night so as to be ready at an early hour to accompany Charly to Maidenhead. Both of them were too nervous and excited to sleep, and they sat talking until late. Tony's name was never mentioned except in connection with the race. Bella seemed content to reminisce about their past years on the farm: the horses they had owned before Abner's financial collapse, her first pony, the coming of Jim and Henry, and rides about the countryside with one or the other as her escort. It was almost, Charly feared, as though she contemplated leaving all the days of her childhood behind.

She thought it was impossible to sleep that night, but suddenly Myra was touching her shoulder. It was barely light, but Ben and Jim must leave at dawn to lead Summer Wind at a quiet walk to the Maidenhead race course.

She dressed hurriedly, donning the rose velvet riding habit. Bella was already awake and met her as she came out into the hall. They were too excited to eat breakfast, Charly feeling sick with anticipation and Bella radiant in her new confidence in the Beautiful Tony.

Henry, who was to stay behind proudly guarding the farm with Ben's musket, had old Bruno and the light chaise waiting at the gate. Tony had arranged to meet them at the track. Kevin, he said, would drive him out in his phaeton. This last had given Charly a measure of comfort. Kevin should be there. After all, he ought to witness her triumph!

Maidenhead, on the east side of Bowery Lane, was the scene of many varied events, sometimes serving as a parade ground. Today it had the atmosphere of a fair. Horses whinnied, dancing in circles about their handlers. People were everywhere, crowding about the track, a bare strip of land a quarter of a mile long set off by railed fencing against which the crowds pressed, jockeying for the best viewpoints. Carriages drawn up along the route provided high seating for those fortunate enough to secure a front row. Charly guided Bruno to a place well back of the starting line where she could see Wind, throwing his head and adding his neighs to the raucous commotion.

It would be a long day, because the races for the untried two-year-olds would be in a series of heats run between the regularly scheduled events, the winners progressively pitted against each other until one reigned supreme. And that one would be Summer Wind.

The horse already was so excited that Jim could hardly

hold him. Tony swung up into the saddle. The long tails of his riding coat parted to reveal a crop stuck into the waistband of his breeches.

"Here now," Ben yelled up at him. "Drop that whip! Don't go striking him or he'll go to pieces!"

Tony, as strung up as the horse, gritted his teeth. "Stand off or he'll trample you. I've got him in control. I know what I'm doing."

He seemed to be right, for Wind, recognizing the familiar hands on his bridle and the weight on his back, began to settle down.

Leaving Bruno tied at a hitching rack near the edge of the grounds, Charly and Bella made their way toward the finish line. As they pushed through the boisterous throng, Bella pointed out Kevin Marlowe on the other side of the track, sitting high above everyone in his preposterous phaeton. He at least had a ringside seat. They managed to squeeze up against the fence about a hundred yards from the end.

Charly hung over the rail as the first two colts came up to the starting line. Wind was to run in the second heat. The flag dropped and the horses charged off in a frantic sprint to the finish, marked by tall white posts held by two officials. More officials in a raised booth watched intently, but no more so than Charly who avidly assessed the merits of the winner, for he would eventually run against Wind.

Wind won his first heat easily, and the next two as well, but the strain showed on both dust-covered horse and rider. Wind had worked himself into a state of near "high-strikes," as Myra would say, but his excitement seemed to add to his speed. Charly, clutching the fence with white-knuckled hands, could hardly keep her feet on the ground, and Bella had quite lost her voice from shouting encouragement.

The final heat was called, with Silas Hawkes's Cyclone as Wind's last opponent. Wind kicked at the other horse as they danced up to the starting line. Tony kept up a steady stream or words directed at him, and not very polite ones judging from the expression on his face.

The flag dropped. Wind plunged and reared instead of lunging forward, and Tony, his temper lost, struck him with the crop. The horse bucked the length of the track and Cyclone was an easy winner.

Charly, numb with shock, hung on the fence. The race—and Deane Farm—were lost.

CHAPTER

Thirteen

Kevin Marlowe climbed down from the precarious perch atop his crane-neck phaeton, from which height he had enjoyed an excellent view of Tony's catastrophe. If that wasn't just like the boy! Time and again he'd nearly combed his brother's hair with a joint stool for losing his temper with an animal. Now he'd see how his pretty bit of frailty took his losing the meet for her sister!

Leaving the carriage in charge of his tiger, he moved toward the group about Mrs. Deane. The horse now stood restlessly chomping on the bit and twisting its head, trying to catch a rein. Tony had dismounted, and a small man with his arm in a sling ran to take the bridle. He was gently pushed aside by a strong-looking young boy, who took the reins from his good hand. Bella ran from her sister's side and began pounding on Tony's back with both clenched fists. Tony, somehow shrunken in size, turned to face his inamorata, who had turned into a veritable virago.

"I heard Ben tell you not to whip him!" she cried. "You knew what would happen! You did it on purpose so we'd lose the race—so I'd have to marry Richard Cranford and set you free! Well, you have your wish. I'll marry him at once!"

She looked about wildly and saw Cranford, who had been watching from the other side of the field, coming toward them. She ran to him, weeping hysterically, and flung herself into his arms. Tony, as white-faced as though she'd struck him, watched as the somewhat startled Cranford accepted his tearful armful and led her away.

Treadwell stood before Mrs. Deane with an unspoken "I told you so" in every line of his stance. "Now will you heed me, Charlotte, and give up this foolishness at once?" Kevin heard him say as he came up with them.

Charlotte stood frozen, her eyes huge and dark in her stricken face as her world collapsed about her. The screaming commotion of the crowd, let alone Treadwell's words, did not appear to penetrate her blank shock. Kevin's lips tightened. His young fool of a brother had known how important this race was to the sisters! Yet all he had talked about had been the distressing habits of the horse and his own ability to handle this most fractious animal. He planned not only to cope but to triumph—for himself, not for the ladies. So much for Tony!

Treadwell had embarked on a long harangue, and Mrs. Deane turned to look up at him, her rigidly erect figure beginning to crumple. Good God, the woman was about to faint! Kevin sauntered over and joined the fray.

"Get off, Treadwell, can you not see you are oversetting the lady?" His massive figure towered before Jonathan, and his lip curled in distaste as he looked the man up and down. Treadwell straightened up as if preparing to square off with him. Kevin simply ignored him, shoving him aside to take his place by Charlotte. He took her arm in a comforting grasp.

"You are in no condition to travel alone, ma'am," he said with a firmness that brooked no argument. "Allow me to escort you back to town. Cranford will see to it that your sister arrives home safely, and my tiger will take your chaise."

He started to lead her away, found he supported the whole of her slight weight, and slipped an arm about her waist to hold her up. She went with him blindly, as if unable to think for herself. *Damn* Tony for his childish temper! He looked over his shoulder and saw his brother still standing irresolute by the lad who was busily unsaddling Wind.

"Go with the men and the horse," he ordered. "See it back to the farm and then come to me at the hotel." Tony met his gaze and nodded dumbly.

While the tiger held the team, Kevin boosted Charly up into the seat of his phaeton. He took the reins, gave the boy his instructions, and then draped a robe over Charlotte's knees. The woman was shivering! With care, he wended his way through the departing crowd and started down Bowery Lane back toward New York City.

As the farms began to give way to closely set houses and they neared the town, Charly roused herself enough to look around. "Oh, no, please!" she managed through a tight throat. "I . . . I do not wish to remain in town. If you would procure me a coach . . . I wish to go to the farm."

"I'll drive you there," he said brusquely. At the next street, he turned and headed back toward Deane Farm. Charlotte relapsed into silence on the high perch seat beside him. Risking a glance away from the rutted road, he looked at her huddled figure. Her even white teeth, he noted, firmly clenched her lower lip. He fought down an impulse to gather her into his arms, ruefully guessing that she would reject such an act. She was possessed of a bravery and strength of will that he had never before encountered in such a tiny female.

And that, if he was honest, was not all that he found attractive about her. At the race meet, he had caught himself watching for her slight form moving about in the crowd. Now, why did he find such pleasure in watching that slim, graceful woman in the rose-colored velvet habit? She had spirit and determination, characteristics he admired—and beauty, too, when she laid aside those beastly buckskins. He remembered the gently rounded curves of her slender figure in the too-large breeches, and the way the ancient jerkin not cut for the fullness of her very feminine form, pulled apart at the top.

Dammed if she didn't look good even in that outfit.

She was certainly not vain nor was she missish. He liked that in a woman, being no dandy himself. Her evening gowns might be elegant, but this was the way she looked her best, in the vastly becoming riding habit she now wore.

Grudgingly, he admitted to himself that he had come to do more than admire the dratted female. But she was an American, with Colonial manners! She would never be accepted by the English *haut ton*—not that she was likely to go to England! He found himself hoping she would not be such a fool as to marry Treadwell. The man was a pompous ass with no sensibility. He hadn't the soul to appreciate real worth in a female.

Cranford was more in her line, a gentleman of wit and worldly wisdom. Why could he not see she was far above and beyond her silly little sister? He would do much better with Charlotte. Any man would. Well, no doubt Cranford would soon realize that. But he was not the man for Charlotte Deane, either. Cranford was a city dandy, a man-about-town. He'd appreciate her beauty but not her real worth, the indomitable spirit, her love for her horses, her willingness to work like a stable-hand to see them succeed— wasted on a man like Cranford.

All at once Kevin found himself disliking Cranford. Why did the man not go back to Philadelphia where he belonged?

He shifted uneasily on the high swaying seat as he steered his team through a section of road almost destroyed by the last rain. What he felt for this woman who sat wrapped in her thoughts beside him was disturbingly warmer than mere friendship. There was something very taking about a female who had a mind, a purpose in life besides the fashion of her gowns and the set of her coiffure. He rather liked her old-fashioned long hair, even fetching when in businesslike braids coiled about her head as today. She was definitely not your everyday female. No, not in the common way at all. There was substance to this lady. A Kate worth the winning . . .

Good God, this wouldn't do! Here he was, trying to extricate Tony from a pretty provincial, and he was falling into the exact same trap!

Determined to break the spell, he searched for a topic of conversation. Anything would do, to knock some sense into his befuddled head and rouse her from her shattered lethargy. He stole another glance at her. The color had begun to seep back into her cheeks and he ventured a light sally.

"I believe we passed the 'Kissing Bridge' just as we left town, and I forgot to collect my toll. Shall I do so now?"

At that, her attention snapped to him. "Indeed you will not!"

"Won't I?"

"Never!"

"Damn," he remarked mildly. "Never?"

For some reason she didn't answer that. "You are entirely too free with your familiarities as it is!" she scolded.

He smiled at her. "Ah, I thought that would awaken you! You have scarcely uttered a word since we left the meet."

"There . . . there has been nothing to say. It is over."

His eyes narrowed as he saw the strain in her face, the effort she put forth to keep her voice calm and matter-of-fact. A lesser female would have given way to hysterics by this time. But then a lesser female would not have driven herself to this point in the first place, risking all for the slim chance of winning.

"I . . . I must thank you for driving me home," she said, as if his comment on her silence reminded her of her manners.

"Nonsense." He almost snapped the word. It was the least he could do for her, for anyone in the state she was in. "A visit to your farm is always a . . . a challenge." He caught her eyeing the faint stains on the knees of his breeches. "Yes, I'm afraid Finch was unable to remove it all. That is very potent mud one encounters in a stable."

She flushed. "I am sorry."

"You needn't be. It was quite my own fault, and I shall have new breeches tomorrow. I found a tailor willing to oblige on short notice." He returned his attention to his team for a few busy minutes as he passed a slow coach. "I have bespoken four pairs," he mused. "I do hope that will be sufficient until I return to England."

"You have only to avoid me, sir." A trace of her spirit returned and he grinned.

"Oh, no. I feel it to be a fair price for a few hours of your company. You cannot deny that so far, you have seen to it that I am not bored."

She turned her face away, still unable to smile.

"Here, now, I merely try to cheer you. All is not lost, you know. This is only one meet. There will be others."

She shook her head, as though not trusting herself to answer for a moment. She drew in a ragged breath. "Not . . . not for me. Mr. Van Bleek will foreclose in a few more months."

"How much do you think you will get for your yearlings?" he demanded bluntly.

"Not nearly enough, now."

"Your mares are good, the best I've seen. You need only a sire with heavier bones and easier disposition."

She appeared to be choking back what sounded suspiciously like a sob. "I cannot wait for a new crop of foals. You knew he granted me that short extension at your request only to finish this race and sell my stock. If Wind had won . . ." She shook her head. "Now all is hopeless."

"Never say that, Mrs. Deane. You will come about. I have observed that you have many friends. Something will turn up."

She looked at him, seeing the strength in his harsh profile. Would he, too, advise her to marry Jonathan? Somehow, that was a very unpleasant thought. She watched him as he drove in silence for a while, a thoughtful expression in his eyes. She felt a sudden urge to admit what she had feared all along and had striven to ignore.

"I know what has defeated me. I've remained blind to a fatal streak passed on to Summer Storm's foals, a wildness in his nature. Wind becomes headstrong, uncontrollable when he is excited. I have tried to convince myself that my yearlings are only high-spirited, but I have seen them let fly at each other in the pasture, beyond mere playfulness."

With consummate skill, he settled a leader who appeared about to shy at a wind-blown branch. "You need a mellow stallion like my Excalibur."

"Of course, I'll ship all my mares to Ireland at once," she agreed and he laughed.

"You know, that is not a bad idea."

Charly managed a smile and found, to her surprise, that she had begun to relax, succumbing to the steadying aura of power and quiet strength that emanated from the broad-shouldered man beside her. She could not help but admire his handling of the ribbons. Trying to force her problems from her mind, she concentrated on his efforts, noting that the management of the precariously high crane-necked carriage required far more skill than the light chaise she was accustomed to driving.

Suddenly, irrationally, she wanted to try her hand at handling his team. Perhaps it was a desperate need to do something to improve her sinking self-image, to prove she could succeed at something, to show this man she was not a total failure. She knew herself to be an excellent whip, perhaps not in the class of the nonesuch now driving his team to an inch, but quite well enough. She'd never driven more than a pair before, but she once had very sporting vehicles at her disposal and high-stepping, spirited horses. All in the past now; since Abner's financial disaster, she'd had only old Bruno between the shafts. But the old skill must remain!

She observed Marlowe's style closely for a mile or so and her certainty grew: she could drive his team. And she needed to prove to herself, as well as to him, that she could do something not every female could. She could not run off to India and recoup her fortune as the man beside her had done when faced with his father's bankruptcy, but she could at least achieve a minor triumph and alleviate a bit of her deep depression.

"May I take the reins?" She felt no compunction in asking this, secure in the confidence of her own ability.

"You most certainly may not!" To her chagrin, he laughed at her.

"Oh, you need have no fear for your team! I'll have you know I can do anything connected with horses, saddled or harnessed."

Maddeningly, he shook his head. "All females are cowhanded," he pronounced. "And even if I were to risk my team, it would most assuredly not be in this vehicle! Only one woman has ever been known to drive one properly: the notorious Lady Archer of London."

Her spirits, though frayed by nerves and despair, began to revive. "Speaking of notorious females . . . !" She began without thinking, knowing only that here was a bone of contention between them, and she intended to have it out—with a battle royal if necessary. "You have certainly gotten upon terms of intimacy with Simone Galbraith!"

Kevin cast her a humorous glance. "She is . . . ah . . . free with her charms."

Charlotte blushed furiously. The odious man! He was telling her outright that Simone Galbraith was a female of easy virtue and that he . . . ! She was unaccustomed to dissembling and, to her growing wrath, his amused gaze followed the play of emotions across her crystal-clear features.

"Oh, sorry. Shocked you, have I? You must know a man of my age is rarely celibate, ma'am."

"Sir, you are no gentleman!"

"No, now. Did I ever say I was? That is my problem. I thought I had explained that to you."

She bit her lip, silenced, furious with herself for allowing her temper to lead her into bringing up this indiscreet turn of conversation. All men had their adventures. Kevin Marlowe's were no more her concern than were those of Richard Cranford or—or Jonathan Treadwell!

Jonathan Treadwell. For the first time, she considered this. He was a full five-and-thirty at least, much the same age as Marlowe. But never, to her recollection, had she heard his name coupled with a lady within or even on the fringes of society. She had heard, of course, of the "holy ground" by St. John's Church and of the loose women who frequented the Battery at night—and even during the day. She knew a lively curiosity. Did Jonathan . . . ? Hurriedly, she turned her thoughts. How dare Kevin Marlowe make her think such things! More than ever, she determined to put him in his place.

At that moment, Kevin slowed his team to turn onto the drive, rousing her from her thoughts. In a very few minutes, he drew his horses up in front of the gate. Looping the reins over the whipstock, he jumped down and walked around the phaeton to help her alight.

Still seething, Charly acted. She would do something to show him! She took up the reins and snapped them over the horses' backs. The startled animals bolted forward, and she drove the equipage in a circle, back to the rutted country road.

She clutched the reins, panicking, as she careened nearly ten feet off the ground in the wildly swaying seat. The horses plunged, next to unmanageable, and each turn nearly overturned the vehicle or tossed her into a ditch. Determined to bring the horses back under control, she held to the road, covering a mile or more before they slowed from a dead run to a canter.

Hoofbeats behind her came closer and closer, sending the team dashing onward as if in a race. She snatched a backward glance and hauled harder on the reins. It was Kevin. He drew abreast, astride one of her horses, riding bareback and with only a halter. He edged his mount near, and reaching out, caught the bit of the left leader. With his consummate skill, he eased the phaeton to a halt.

"What the hell do you think you're doing?" he panted. "Damn well trying to wreck my rig?"

Reaction from the terror-filled ride left her shaking so she could hardly speak, but she wasn't to be sworn at! And offense, she remembered, was the best defense.

"You fool!" she cried. "No saddle and no bridle! That colt is only half broken! You could have been killed!"

"Me!" he exploded. "You were near as the devil dashed to death on that last curve!" Without mincing words, he proceeded to comb her hair in fine style for taking such a chance, calling her a blasted female idiot, a hoyden, and a mannerless American savage. "I was right about you the very first time I saw you!" he finished, his voice choked with anger.

"I drove them, didn't I?" she shouted back.

"No, they drove you! If my horses weren't so well trained, you would have overturned. Now get the hell down from there!"

To her surprise, she found herself obeying him meekly, as fast as her trembling limbs allowed. As he turned away to tie the haltered colt to the rear of the phaeton, she stared in horror at the inevitable result of riding a sweating horse bareback.

"Oh . . . oh, dear!" she managed to gasp, then helplessly,

in a further reaction to her emotions, she gave way to a fit of the giggles.

"What now?" He followed her gaze. "Hell and the devil confound it! My last pair, ruined! Lady, I can't afford to know you!"

"You . . . you didn't have to come after me!"

"Dammit, I didn't come after you. I came after my phaeton! Do you realize it would take the better part of a year to get a replacement here from England?"

He didn't mention replacing *her*! Suddenly, unreasonably, she was so furious that she slapped him and drew her hand back for a second blow. She never got the chance. He caught her wrist and pure fury shone in his eyes. She recoiled. Would he strike her back? Instead, he yanked her into his arms and kissed her roughly, bruising her lips and crushing her ribs.

She clung to him, wondering hazily why the kiss of a man she despised should completely overthrow all her senses. Against her will she returned the kiss in a manner that gave no doubt as to her feelings, surrendering to the passion and fury of the atmosphere about them, knowing only that for this one moment, she gave her all.

He released her suddenly, as if her lips had burned him. Fairly throwing her back up into the high seat, he drove her back to the farm in a dead silence she was afraid to break.

CHAPTER

Fourteen

Kevin Marlowe strode into his rooms at the Tontine House, striving to whip his anger to a white heat. Only by maintaining his wrath at that abominable horse lady could he keep his churning emotions on a rational keel. Another sensation threatened to overbalance him, one that he could not tolerate for a moment. By sheer force of will, he blanked from his mind the memory of her warm body trembling in his arms, the softness of her lips crushed beneath his . . .

This would not do! Not for so much as a single second! He had achieved his purpose, and his business here was done. Tony's regrettable affair with the American chit was broken up. She had thrown him over for Cranford.

Why did this last give him an extra measure of satisfaction? The removal of Cranford from the lists seeking Charlotte Deane's favor shouldn't affect him in the least! At least she wouldn't marry Treadwell, of that he felt sure. But that was beside the point. He and Tony were free to return to England and by the first packet! He'd best go to Boston at once and see his shipping agent. In fact, the sooner he got himself out of New York City, the better.

A long sea voyage was just what he needed to get his mind off . . . off things. With luck, it would storm all the way, which would suit his mood to a T. What a fool he'd been to kiss that damned female again! It wasn't as if he didn't know how it would tear him apart to let her go. He'd already experienced that rending sensation of loss once before, in the pleasure garden outside that gazebo. Only this time, it had been ten times worse. Charlotte Deane was a witch!

That earlier time, the delectable Mrs. Galbraith had helped. But he wasn't going to her. The very idea left him cold. It would be a pallid remedy for the fever that gripped him now as he felt again that soft, slim figure filling his arms.

Good God, there was nothing for it but to run! He was not about to succumb to some silly infatuation! He opened his door and bellowed for Finch, then remembered he had to wait for that confounded tailor to deliver his new breeches. He cursed the idiocy that had prompted him to pack an inadequate wardrobe—now all ruined by that damnable female! No use to remind himself that he had not intended to remain in America above a week; he should have known he'd need more clothing. The hapless Finch should have warned him! And where was the man?

The door burst open and not Finch, but Tony, fairly flung himself into the room. He threw himself down into a chair with such violence that the fragile piece of furniture threatened to collapse beneath him.

"It is all over town!" he declared, savagely.

"What is?" Kevin snapped back, not overly interested.

"About Isabella accepting Cranford. I have just come from the Binghams; they say that everyone is talking about it." He rose with such force that the hapless chair teetered dangerously. "Please, Kev, arrange passage back to England for me when you go! America is a devil of a place! I want to go home!"

Home. Tony was not the only one engulfed by this longing. Charly sat on the broad piazza that ran the length of the front of her farmhouse. Never before had she realized just how very much she loved the square wooden building with its high stone basement, surrounded by her garden. Her home. And now she was about to lose it.

She sat dry-eyed. Tears and despair gained one nothing! She was not going to give up, no matter how dire the circumstances. It was not in her nature. Her mind worried her problem like a dog with a bone, turning it over and over, searching for a trace of meat.

Was there one ray of hope? Wind might have lost the meet ultimately, but did he not prove the speed of his bloodline? Hope surged through her. Surely, anyone who saw the way her horse had won all the previous races before losing to Silas's Cyclone must have been impressed by his potential! Her yearlings might yet command a price sufficient to get her out of her difficulties!

Then reality closed back in on her, shattering her illusions. She could not forget Wind's tantrum at the gate, the reason he lagged so far behind at the start. No one else would forget it, either. He might have proved his speed, but he also proved his wild temperament. Not every horseman had the patience and ability of Ben Stokes, and an unmanageable racehorse was worse than one lacking in speed. No one would be flocking to Deane Farm to buy yearlings who might turn out as intractable as Wind.

She lowered her face into her hands, refusing to give in to misery. She was not defeated yet, not until Pieter Van Bleek actually came and foreclosed.

She forced her mind away from her problems, but found this provided her no respite. Thoughts of Kevin Marlowe intruded, unwelcome and unsettling. Again, she felt the strength of his arms and the heat of that kiss. Had she been insulted—or desired? She couldn't decide. Of one thing only could she be sure. His patient wrath at her behavior overrode all. Now that Bella had cast aside her Beautiful Tony for Cranford's stability, she'd never see him or his brother again. The Marlowes were gone from her life, and she was glad! Glad! So why this vast depression when all her thoughts should be concentrated on reconstructing her own life?

Rising, she smoothed down the skirt of her rose-velvet habit and strode inside for more suitable farm garments, ignoring a hard, ice-cold lump that had once been the heart in her breast.

* * *

Charly tried to resume her normal activities the next day, but matters at the farm were not the same and never would be. The feeling of excitement, of possible peril, was gone. And so was the underlying feeling of hope. All waited for the inevitable, for a summons or visit from Mr. Van Bleek.

Jim and Henry wanted to abandon their nightly guard duty on the horses, declaring they needed their sleep. Although they did not voice the opinion out loud, Charly could guess their reasoning. No further intervention to ruin her was necessary. Wind had lost the meet. They had managed their downfall, all on their own.

Charly explained the need for protecting her final resources, the yearlings and mares that must go on the block to pay off Van Bleek in the very near future. The boys suggested replacing the trip rope and perhaps a few of the other traps, but their earlier enthusiasm had vanished.

The morning brought new worries. After Wind's strenuous exercise of the day before, he needed light riding to loosen his muscles and keep him from stiffening, but Ben's shoulder was by no means mended. He had been damaged too many times in a long career devoted to the taming of large, high-spirited animals. He would not be able to ride for yet a very long while, and Wind would get no exercise.

"I'll ride him for you, Mrs. Deane," Jim offered, though somewhat dubiously.

Charly hesitated, then shook her head. "I need you whole, Jim, in one piece and able to take over much of Ben's work."

She walked away before the lad could argue. It would be too easy to give in; then who knew what disaster might happen! It dawned on her that she missed Tony's visits. He was always cheerful, laughing, teasing, and joking with Ben and Jim. Even stolid Henry had remarked that it was fun when Mr. Marlowe came out to ride. The men liked Tony. And, what was worse, she acknowledged that she had come to like him, too.

And thinking of Tony... She had been neglecting Bella of late, concerned only with Summer Wind and her farm. And now she stood to lose all. She had best return to town and concentrate on her little sister, try to help her through this terrible period.

Of one thing she was sure. Bella would receive no sympathy from Aunt Augusta for breaking off with Tony and rashly accepting Richard Cranford's former offer. Knowing their aunt, she most likely must have been thrown into transports at the announcement. And General Parks with her. Charly shuddered, envisioning the scene, with Bella miserably unhappy and too furious to admit it.

Upon her return to Beaver Street, Charly found that she had been correct in her assessment. Neither Richard Cranford nor General Parks were there, but the house bore the atmosphere of her aunt's barely contained excitement.

"Charly, we must give a ball at once," Aunt Augusta informed her the moment she entered the drawing room. "We shall celebrate this betrothal in prime style!" With rare restraint, not one word did she utter on the subject of Charlotte's farm.

Charly had a chance to observe her sister and her affianced husband late that afternoon when Cranford came to tea, and her heart sank. Richard's eyes held a haunted look, but he disguised this gallantly and tried to play up to a pale-faced Bella. The girl's laughter was artificial and brittle. Between the two of them, they valiantly maintained the fiction of happiness. Neither, Charly guessed shrewdly, wanted to upset their delighted elders.

As if sensing a certain reluctance on the part of both principals, Aunt Augusta hurriedly forged ahead with wedding plans, ably assisted by General Parks. Talk in the house for the next few days was of nothing else. Even Charly became wrapped up in them, for Bella herself seemed determined to carry it through, and as quickly as possible. Once again, a wall seemed to separate the sisters, and Charly, try as she might, was unable to induce Bella to confide in her.

With almost unseemly haste, the evening of the announcement ball arrived. It seemed impossible that an entire week had passed since the disastrous race meet. In the back of her mind, Charly wondered why Pieter Van Bleek had not yet called upon her, but the round of preparations kept her too busy to dwell on the subject. Indeed, she couldn't bear to think of it, for Ben already was preparing a list of invitations to the auction of her stock. All but Zephyr would go on the block. Only a complete dispersal would save her land.

The betrothal ball, without doubt, was the worst party Charly had ever attended. Augusta, either not being acquainted with all the ramifications of the situation, or else possessed of a perverse sense of deviltry, had invited Simone Galbraith, and she came. With a false smile fixed on her pretty, pouting lips, she congratulated Cranford and wished Bella happy. But if looks could kill . . . !

Neither Tony nor Kevin were invited, for which Charly could only be glad. She kept repeating this to herself but found it strangely unreassuring. And why should she care? Rumor had it that both had left New York City. And why, when she heard of it, should that news cause the pit of her stomach to drop sickeningly?

For once, Jonathan Treadwell did not propose several times during the evening, but this situation did nothing to cheer her. His attitude appeared to be that he no longer had the need—she was his for the taking. He might only stand up with her twice, but his manner was more possessive than ever. He took charge of her as though it was his right, and Charly was too demoralized to care.

And then Pieter Van Bleek, as an old friend of the general's, arrived and Charly felt that her evening of unrelieved misery had become complete. To her surprise, he greeted her warmly, congratulating her on her sister's excellent alliance.

Charly bit her lip and tried to smile back. "We . . . we are delighted, of course," she managed.

"An excellent gentleman," Mr. Van Bleek went on. "Though I never thought he'd be one to fall into the parson's mousetrap, but there you are. Quite a taking little thing, your sister."

The strain was too much for Charly. This might be a social occasion, but the business matter that hung between them was too great to be ignored. Taking the proverbial bull by the horns, she met his gaze squarely. "Mr. Van Bléek, I fear we have a matter to discuss."

"No hurry, my dear." He patted her hand in an avuncular manner.

Shock left her momentarily speechless. "You . . . you will be repaid," she assured him, after a moment.

"Of course, so I have been informed. I am quite pleased for you, Mrs. Deane, quite pleased."

Charly blinked. "I . . . thank you," she stammered. Unsteadily she moved away, not knowing what to make of his response. He must have heard that Summer Wind lost the meet! Why was he not demanding instant repayment as he had threatened when he heard of Summer Storm's death? Certainly, he had allowed a few months after the race for her to sell off her yearlings, but still . . .

Across the room, she met Jonathan's gaze, and her cheeks flamed. Jonathan, and his arrogant assumption again! Of course, there could be no other answer. He, and only he, could have reassured Pieter Van Bleek. Why could Jonathan not realize that she would never marry him? But what else was there for her to do . . . ?

Unable to face the crowded room, Charly slipped down the hall. Her late father's study had not been opened up as a card room this evening, and should provide her with a haven. To her surprise, the door stood slightly ajar. As she started to push it open, the sound of a hushed female voice reached her.

". . . have you forgotten our understanding so quickly?"

Charly hesitated, then turned to leave. She recognized the dulcet tones of Simone Galbraith, and she had no desire to listen to the notorious woman making her assignations! The next voice, though, stopped her.

"My marriage to Miss Hanley is one of my uncle's ideas," Richard Cranford said. "I might add I only offered for her at his instigation."

There followed the sounds of movement and the rustling of satin, and Charly, peeping in at the door, saw that he had drawn the unprotesting Simone into his arms.

"I cannot, in honor, withdraw from the engagement," Cranford went on, "but I do not see why that—or my

marriage, for that matter!—should make any difference in
our arrangement.''

"Indeed, why should it?" Simone Galbraith murmured.

Charly waited to hear no more. This man was not for
Bella! Fairly seething, she hurried back to the ballroom. The
fatal public announcement would not be made for yet
another half hour, at midnight. She would put a stop to it!

"Aunt Augusta!" Firmly, she ousted Anabel Brougham
from her aunt's side. "Dearest, I must have a word with
you."

"Where are you taking me?" Augusta demanded as
Charly wheeled her chair to an unoccupied corner.

In very few words, Charly poured out the tale of the
scene she had just witnessed into her aunt's shocked ears.

"No!" Augusta moaned weakly. "You are quite right.
Oh, Charly, how I had hoped . . . ! But that is neither here
nor there." She sat erect in her chair. "Bella must cry off.
Oh, the poor child!"

But Charly was not so sure she considered her "poor."
Bella's acceptance of Richard Cranford had been done in a
moment of fury, and almost certainly regretted at once.
Bella, alone of the household, had shown no interest in all
the wedding plans. Had she been less brokenhearted over
Tony, Charly guessed she would have called off her impetu-
ous engagement almost immediately. But without her Tony,
Bella no longer seemed to care what became of her.

This thought was confirmed a very few minutes later. The
country dance came to an end and Bella left the floor, her
face still pale and drawn. Charly caught her and led her
gently aside.

Faced with her innocent little sister, Charly suddenly
found herself at a loss to explain Cranford's perfidy. She
hesitated, then put out a tentative feeler. "Bella, I . . . I feel
you should cry off from this engagement, before it is
announced," she ventured.

"Why?" Bella asked, hopelessness dulling her voice.

"I don't think Richard would make you a very good
husband. He . . . he is not really the marrying kind, you
know.''

"Is he not?" Bella shrugged. "I thought you wanted me to marry him."

Charly grasped her cold hands. "I want you to be happy, and so does Aunt Augusta. You will find that she will not blame you for crying off. Please, do so, dearest. I cannot bear you to be so unhappy."

Bella raised eyes filled with tears. "I . . . I have no wish to marry anyone," she lied valiantly.

"Then tell Richard at once. Would you wish me to come with you?"

Bella nodded, clutching Charly's hand as if it were a lifeline.

Richard, upon being informed that his betrothed had changed her mind, made a suitable attempt to look sorry. Neither sister was deceived, for his relief was evident. He took Bella's hand, kissed it thankfully, and assured her that he wished her happy always. They parted upon warmer terms than had characterized the brief period of their unofficial engagement.

To Charly's surprise, not even General Parks seemed unduly concerned by the turn of events.

"I was afraid this would happen," he said calmly, when Augusta brought him to task for his nephew's shocking conduct. "The boy is just like I was myself at that age, an incorrigible rake. He will be far happier as a bachelor."

"With his Simone," Augusta said tartly, not pretending to be shocked. There was no doubt, though, that she forgave both him and Cranford. She had ever a soft spot for a rake, especially an old one.

When the last of the guests departed, Charly retired to her bed to lie awake into the early hours of the morning. Perhaps she should take Bella home for a few days' rest, to recover from the emotional trauma of the past week. They needed a respite from town—and the gossips—that would arise after the ball, for no one gave such an affair on a week's notice without a reason.

She rose early, still bleary-eyed but anxious to get underway. When she peeped in on Bella she found the girl still asleep. Restless, she made her way down to the breakfast parlor. Contenting herself with a piece of toast and a cup of tea, she sat at the table and stared off into space, trying to see a solution to their difficulties.

From this she was disturbed by Jensen, who informed her that Mr. Anthony Marlowe was below and desired to speak to her alone. Charly stared at the butler blankly, then swallowed hard. Hadn't she heard that both Marlowe brothers had left for Boston? Could this mean . . . ? She stood quickly, filled with a wild surmise, and hurried down to join him. Did he bring a message from Kevin? And why was she trembling like a silly schoolroom miss?

Getting a firm hold on herself, she entered the room quietly. Tony turned from the window and stepped forward, somewhat diffidently, and took the hand she offered.

"To what do I owe the pleasure of this call, Tony?" she asked. "I had thought you in Boston."

"Kevin went on ahead. I . . . I have stayed in town." He appeared disconcerted, as if he had no idea what to say next.

Charly's heart sank. His visit had nothing to do with Kevin. She seated herself on the sofa and gestured Tony toward the chair opposite. He took it, still looking uncharacteristically ill at ease.

"I . . . oh *damn*!" he exclaimed hotly. "I beg pardon, Mrs. Deane." He bounced up from his seat. "I . . . I heard from the Binghams, who were here last night. Bella and Cranford did not announce their engagement. Is it true?" He ended on a note of such forlorn hope that Charly's gentle heart went out to him.

"Yes, they decided that they should not suit."

Tony took a deep breath. "I . . . I have been staying in town on the chance that Bella might forgive me. I . . . oh, surely you must know! I have formed a lasting passion for your sister!" He shook his head, as if that knowledge still amazed him. "I love her, Mrs. Deane. So I have come to beg your permission to pay my addresses to Bella in the proper style."

A lump rose in Charly's throat, almost choking her. Bella would be happy . . . Charly almost forgot that Tony was penniless without the backing of his brother. Suddenly, all that mattered was Bella, heartbroken and miserable, whose love was in fact returned ...

Then a new selfish fear arose. Would Tony return to England, taking Bella with him? Charly bit her lip, unable to bear the thought. Was she to lose everything she loved at once? Her farm, her horses, her sister, and—and something else she refused to recognize. But for Bella's happiness, she could not allow any of that to weigh with her.

Thrusting her own misery aside, she reached out impulsively, taking Tony's hand. Hope transformed his handsome face.

"Oh, Tony," she said. "Bella ..." She broke off in consternation as she remembered Kevin's reason for coming to America. Had she the right, knowing of Tony Marlowe's prior committment in England, even though made by Kevin on his behalf, to consent to this union and overset his elder brother's hard-won arrangement?

"Mrs. Deane?" Tony asked. The pressure of his fingers recalled her.

"Tony, I ... I *cannot* give you my blessing!" she cried. "Not yet."

His mouth dropped open. "But—"

"No, please, Tony. Listen. Remember your brother's plans, everything he has worked for. You are betrothed already in England. You must gain your release and then Kevin's permission, before I can give mine."

"And will we have yours, then?" he demanded, pressing her hand even tighter.

She nodded. "But *only* if you can convince your brother. And I am very much afraid you may never succeed at that."

Tony groaned loudly, sharing her belief. "I care nothing for London society! Mrs. Deane, I would give up everything, including Kev's fortune, for the love of Bella!"

Charly felt a tiny pang of jealousy for her little sister, who had found her love. "You must not marry out of hand," she asserted. "It would alienate your brother forever, and I cannot let that happen." She disengaged her fingers, which were almost numb from Tony's grip, and stood. "Perhaps if I could talk to him ..."

"Would you?" Tony asked, his expression eager. He

sank back into the chair, shaking his head. "Not that it will do any good. Nothing will change Kev's mind, not once he has taken a maggot into his head."

Charly was not listening. She had made an excuse to see Kevin again, and she was startled by the rush of elation this thought brought. "I . . . I will do my best to reconcile your brother to the idea, though, knowing his freely and often expressed opinion of Americans . . ." On the whole, she saw little hope. But she had to try, for Bella's sake as well as her own. "Where is he, Tony?"

"He went to Boston to see his shipping agent. I . . . I expected him to send for me before now." All at once he brightened. "Do you know, he may well have given up on me! I refused to accompany him at the last moment, you see. Maybe he has gone back to Ireland!" He brightened perceptibly, warming to this theme. "You must know he can never be separated long from his Excalibur."

Charly sat down abruptly as her legs refused to support her. Kevin, leaving America . . . not coming back to New York . . . A peculiar weakness assailed every part of her, leaving her dizzy at this shattering blow. And the extent of her reaction, she realized with horror, could only mean one thing. She had fallen hopelessly in love with the impossible Kevin Marlowe.

And what of him? Surely there had been signs that he was not altogether indifferent, that his regard toward her had been animated. That last kiss . . . Had he not been as overwhelmed as she? How could he leave without seeing her one last time, without giving her a chance? Did social ambition mean that much to him? Could he not come to love her more than his horse?

But it was more than just his Excalibur. She knew how she felt about Zephyr and Deane Farm. How much more must a man feel, with an estate handed down through the generations and the challenge of reestablishing his ancient family in the eyes of the only society he revered?

"What do you say, Mrs. Deane?" Tony's voice penetrated the shrouding fog about her.

"Say?" she asked hazily. "About what?"

"Give us your blessing! If Kev has given up and gone home—"

"Then you must follow him to Ireland and get his formal permission. No, don't argue with me, Tony. A fine thing it would be in me to give my permission when I *know* your brother has expressly forbidden the marriage."

"That will take half a year!" he cried, dismayed.

"I see no other way. Look, Tony, you are officially engaged to this female that your brother has found. Whatever your feelings on the subject may be, consider hers . . . and Bella's! I cannot permit you to see my sister again until you are completely free of all other commitments."

Tony looked truculent, but Charly remained firm. At last, convinced that she would not be moved from what he could only feel—and freely express—to be an unreasonable position, he took his leave.

Charly sank down upon the sofa, fighting back a desire to succumb to tears. The sooner she left the city, with all its bustle and gossips and handsome young Marlowes, the better! She would escape to the peace of her farm, and enjoy the last few days that she would possess it, for even that would be taken from her all too soon.

CHAPTER
Fifteen

After nearly a week on the road, Kevin Marlowe guided his phaeton over the causeway at the Neck and entered Boston proper. Driving oneself was a very different thing from traveling while leaning back against the squabs inside a well-sprung coach, and he was road-weary and irritable. Only his intention to ship the phaeton back to England with him had led to his bringing it along.

He was alone. Finch and his tiger had been left in New York to follow by stage when sent for. Marlowe did not wish to subject the boy to an arduous journey clinging to the rear step of the phaeton. Besides, he needed the space for his baggage. Finch he left because the man was poor company on a tedious trip.

He'd had a long time to think during his solitary ride over the dusty, rutted track, and ever his mind had revolved like a wheel, circling one subject. Leaving New York City by Bowery Lane, which eventually became the Lower Post Road to Boston, he had by necessity passed Deane Farm and felt a tug at his very core that frightened him. Unable, even now, to shake off the sensation, he scarcely noted the street urchins who whooped and chased after his fantastic equipage.

Driving up South End, Orange Street, and Newbury, Kevin drew in at the sign of the Lion on Marlborough. It was late afternoon and he was bone-tired. Morning would do for visiting his shipping agent. After divesting himself of his travel-stained clothing and putting down a hot meal, he wandered out into the street to stretch his cramped legs and attempt once more to sort out his troubled thoughts.

The familiar sounds and odors of the busy seaport assailed his senses: the smells of hot tar, fish, and salt brine, the blasts from the tin horns of peddlers, and the clatter of wagon wheels and horses' hooves on the cobbles. He drew a deep breath, adding boiling soap, drying spices and a brewery to his inventory.

He drifted toward Cornhill. Absently he passed the Old South Meeting House and turned down Water Street. A few long strides brought him to Pudding Lane and, involuntarily, he cut across it to King Street and headed down toward the Long Wharf.

No less than his own confusion, Tony's attitude toward his young New York conquest puzzled him. He had never known Tony to persist in a flirtation for so long. Could it be the boy's heart was more deeply involved than he realized? And only Tony's heart . . . ? He kicked irritably at an innocent weed striving for existence among the cobbles. Was he himself to be sent to grass by a little straw-haired stable hand?

He had to admit the Deane woman had fair given him a leveler, but he was not such a cod's head as to saddle himself with a shrew who would fling the morning coffee over him if he failed to greet her properly!

The creak of ships rubbing against the dock pierced his consciousness. He glanced up, aware for the first time of his surroundings. Without thought, he had walked along the Long Wharf toward the office of his shipping agent and he now stood before it. Lamplight shone from its one window. For a moment he stared up at it, uncomprehending. Now, why had he come here?

With a certainty that astounded him, Kevin realized that his mind had made up itself. He shrugged. There was, he saw, only one way to escape the feeling of hopeless depression that threatened to overwhelm him whenever he relaxed his thoughts. It had come to this. Only one thing to do. He mounted the two steps to his agent's door, went inside, and did it.

Charly hadn't expected her ultimatum to sit well with her volatile sister, and it didn't. Bella had a deal to say on the subject, but Charly remained firm.

"We know nothing of his titled lady in England," she said. "For all we know, she is quite attached to Tony and it is beyond anything that the man should cry off. And on such a pretext!—that he has run away to another country rather than be wed to her!"

"Tony says he does not even know her!" Bella stormed. "Kevin arranged the whole affair. Tony saw her only once, and he says she was toplofty and condescending. It was to be strictly a marriage of convenience; she wanted only his brother's fortune!"

"In that case . . ." Charly vacillated. If the lady was truly so mercenary. . . . "But still the situation must be settled. Until Tony has seen his brother, I will do nothing."

Another thought strengthened Charly's resolve. Tony had no money of his own, and she herself might soon lose her all. What would the young couple live on if Kevin became angry and refused to countenance the marriage?

She could not, in good conscience, give her consent to the marriage with Kevin so opposed. It would be little more than a betrayal. Holding firm to his wishes was the one last thing she could do for him—the one last link in the chain that bound her to him, but that meant nothing to Bella, who now resorted to a torrent of weeping.

It was too much for Charly. "If Tony does go home to Ireland, and then returns, free of his engagement, I will no longer withhold my permission," she promised.

This momentarily halted Bella's tears, but they returned a minute later. "If . . . if Tony once leaves America, his brother will prevent him from ever returning to me! I know he will!" she cried. Just how Kevin might do this she did not venture a guess.

Charly sighed. She had no answer for her unhappy sister. And none for herself. Oh, but she was a fool! How could she have let herself fall in love with Kevin Marlowe simply because he was everything she had ever dreamed of?

Like Bella, she knew there could be only one man for her, for all others fell too short of her ideal. She would rather die a single widow than give herself to anyone else. No, Bella would not be the only one heartbroken if Tony was forced to return to England.

Now that was a defeatist way of looking at things! The world was not at an end. If only she could accept Jonathan, close her eyes to his shortcomings, and force herself into a loveless marriage with the wealthy merchant, she would be able to pay off Van Bleek and buy the stallion she needed to continue. A heavy-boned one. But then she wouldn't need the horse, for Jonathan would never permit his wife to continue running a racing stable. Dead end. Whoever it was who had set out to destroy Deane Farm—and her—had succeeded.

And who could it have been? Once more, Charly turned her thoughts to this puzzle. There had been Bentley's offer for her land. The town was expanding rapidly, as he had said. Could her acres now be so valuable? And Van Bleek. Could he want her land more than his money? The amount still owed was nowhere near the actual value of her property. Could he be behind the shooting of Summer Storm that began her series of misfortunes and then the attempts to injure Summer Wind? Would she ever know?

The following day was taken up with preparations for a party that Aunt Augusta pronounced necessary to welcome her nieces back to town. At first, Augusta had felt it to be indelicate to invite General Parks, his nephew Richard Cranford, and the beguiling Simone Galbraith. But life in town had become dreadfully flat with the Marlowe brothers out of favor. The temptation of watching Cranford flirt with his mistress and seeing if he had the nerve to face Charly and Bella proved too much for her.

To her intense satisfaction, Cranford came, escorting his Simone. And to Charly's satisfaction, Bella showed neither embarrassment nor restraint. The girl greeted them both unaffectedly, putting a period to any ill-natured gossip that might otherwise have run rampant.

Jonathan Treadwell also attended, for he was still Augusta's prime favorite. He immediately cornered Charly, and his conversation did not please her in the least.

He wasted no time in proposing. Instead, and without preamble, he informed her of the plans he had made for their wedding, where they would live, that Bella would be left with Augusta, and that they would dispose of her farm at once.

Charly heard him out in cold silence. There were many women, she supposed, who would be thrilled by such high-handed treatment, seeing it as a sign of strength in a man. She saw it as a sign of pomposity.

"Jonathan!" She interrupted his flow of words. "I want to keep my farm. I must pay off Mr. Van Bleek in only a few more months. If I agreed to marry you, would you advance me the money?"

"You cannot be thinking of going on with this foolishness!" he exploded. "No female has any business in horse racing. It is not seemly, and I will not have you playing at being a stable hand for another day!"

"Playing, Jonathan?" Charly raised her eyebrows. "I do not consider it a game. And I was making a success of it, you know! If only Summer Storm had not been killed, I would not now be in this sad position!"

"It was a stroke of luck for you that someone shot that horse! Sheer luck, the bullet getting him behind the ear like that and not merely winging him!"

Sheer luck? It had been a deliberate act! Someone meant that the horse should be killed and she ruined! She could only be glad that she had guarded the fact that she had such an enemy, or Van Bleek would have foreclosed before now . . . She stared at Jonathan. She *had* kept the secret close. The story had been put about that Storm was killed by a hunter's stray bullet. She had made no mention to Jonathan of where the bullet had struck.

"How did you know where he was hit?" she asked, her voice deadly quiet. "Who told you? I know I didn't. And he was buried before you had the news!"

"I . . ." Jonathan flushed. "Why, you must have told me! How else should I know?"

She shook her head slowly, rising to her feet. "I never did," she whispered. "And unless the person who shot him told you, then——"

"My dear Charlotte!"

"*You* killed him!"

"Now really, Charlotte——!"

"You set out to ruin me!" Her voice rose, filled with the certainty of her discovery.

Realizing he had given himself away, Treadwell began to bluster. "You would not marry me, else! I had to do it! And even you must admit it was for your own good. The beast was vicious——he killed your husband and might have killed you! There was no other way to force you to give up your ridiculous ideas!"

Charlotte stared at him in disbelief. It had been Jonathan all the time. And he was serious! He honestly thought he had done it for the best! Unable to bear facing him for another moment, she turned her back and walked away without a word. She would never be able to forgive him!

Slowly, anger began to drown her feeling of defeat. She would show Jonathan! Nothing was ever gained by giving in to an unhappy fate. She tried to pull herself together. She must decide what had to be done to salvage at least her land from the wreckage. She would keep Bruno and Zephyr, but the other horses would have to go. Surely all would not be lost, if she could just save the land.

During the next week Bella elected to remain in town, and Charly hadn't the heart to deprive her of Tony's company. Only too soon, Kevin would carry him away. Shattered after her confrontation with Jonathan, Charly felt she could no longer attend the round of social functions where she'd have to face him. She returned to the farm to consult with Ben, for the day of the auction would soon arrive.

On her first day home, she wandered out to the pasture area and stood by the fence watching the new colt. He was even lighter boned than she had thought, far more so than Summer Wind. Confound that Kevin Marlowe! Why must he be right? Zephyr's foal would never make it as a racing stallion.

Ben came up and leaned on the rail fence beside her. "He's growing at a fair clip, Mrs. Deane." Thoughtfully he leaned down, pulled a blade of grass, and began to chew it.

"We're going to make it, Ben! I don't know how, yet, but I won't lose this place!"

"That's the spirit, Mrs. Deane. Now, losing that meet was a bit of a leveler, but we aren't down and out, not by a long ways. We've still the auction, you know."

They fell silent. Both knew that Wind's vicious display at the race had lowered the value of Storm's line.

Charly turned away from the fence and with dragging steps returned to the house. As she reached the back door, a carriage turned off the lane and up the drive. Aunt Augusta's coachman, she realized, and hurried forward. As the vehicle pulled to a halt, the door flew open and Bella jumped down. Without speaking, she ran to Charly and threw her arms about her neck.

"Bella! What has happened?" Charly held her off, trying to see her face.

"I . . . I was not happy in town, so I have come home," she answered. Her eyes didn't meet Charly's, and her manner seemed somewhat evasive.

Charly frowned. Bella acted nervous, and a sort of haunted excitement lurked in her blue eyes, as though she had come to some highly dramatic decision and intended to live the part to the hilt.

"Have you come for a last look at Deane Farm before we lose it all?" Charly asked, wondering if the role might be that of a martyr.

Bella burst out weeping, her usual mode of late. "Oh, Charly," she wailed between sobs. "C-can you forgive me? This is all my fault!"

"Good God, how could it be?"

"I . . . I have only been thinking of myself, not of you. My place is here, by your side. I realize now why you don't want me to marry. You need me, and I shouldn't leave you. I'll never forgive myself!" She blew her nose on an inadequate scrap of lace. "Oh, Charly, what am I to do?"

"Well, first off, don't act like a silly goose!" Charly gave the girl a tight squeeze, then released her. "We shall survive, both of us, and you must live your own life! I'll not have you making sacrifices for me. I'll come about, you'll see."

Charly lay awake that night for hours, finally drifting off to weary sleep near dawn, and it was late when she finally roused herself. Bella was nowhere about but she felt no concern. Her sister was probably out in the yard talking to Ben. As a child, Bella had always gone to him with her troubles. Charly dressed in a hurry. There were plans to be made, and Bella and Ben might as well be in on their making. When she went out into the paddock area in search of them, she found Ben alone, repairing a piece of harness.

"Is Bella around?" Charly asked. She looked about, still not anxious. If not with Ben, she fully expected her sister to be at the mare's pasture, inspecting the new foal.

"I've not seen her this morning, Mrs. Deane," Ben replied. With care, he set another stitch into the leather.

Suddenly, unaccountably, Charly was afraid. Turning, she ran back to the house, up the stairs to Bella's room and threw open the door. The bed was badly rumpled, obviously slept in, but her wardrobe stood open, and her bandboxes, her warm pelisse, and some of her gowns were missing.

A sealed note rested on Bella's dressing table where her brushes once lay. With trembling hands, Charly tore it open and read the tearstained message. Tony, Bella wrote in an agitated hand, had come for her at dawn. He could not live without her, nor she without him. She knew Jonathan would care for her dearest Charly if the worst came to pass, and as she herself was just an added burden, she was eloping with the man she loved. Please, please forgive her.

Charly sank down onto the bed, overcome by despair. She was truly alone. Only now did she realize how much of her brave front was based on her absorption in Bella, in Bella's social season, the need to support her, and to receive her support in return. And Bella had deserted her.

This proved to be the last straw! It was outside of enough, her utter undoing. Abandoning all pretense, she threw herself down on the bed and gave in to an orgy of weeping that put Bella's dramatic tears to shame.

Below her, a door slammed; voices and heavy footsteps sounded in the hall. Charly's head came up. Bella and Tony? Could they have come back to her? Shakily, she came to her feet.

"Bella?" she called.

The footsteps came quickly up the stairs. Charly glanced at the mirror, mopped at her wet face and reddened eyes, but there was nothing she could do about her puffy face. Nor did she care. All that mattered . . .

The door swung wide and Kevin Marlowe stood on the threshold. At this of all times!

"Good God, what's toward?" he demanded.

Charly tried to speak and could not command her voice. She took a deep steadying breath. How could she tell him about Bella and Tony? The destruction of all his hopes?

Too overset to think, she ran to him and he caught her frantic hands. "Here, now, tell me all about it. Quietly, love. Is it only your sister?"

"Kevin, they have eloped." She whirled away, grabbing up Bella's crumpled note. "Just see."

Kevin eyed the sheet critically. "Her penmanship is sadly wanting."

This had the result for which he aimed. Charly stamped her foot.

"Oh, do be serious! Only read what she says!" She waited, trembling while he worked his way through the straggling words. "She . . . she says I could marry Jonathan!" she wailed, voicing Bella's crowning iniquity.

"Well, if that is not the height of idiocy!" Kevin pulled her down on the edge of the bed and sat beside her. "I've never heard anything more foolish." He kissed the tips of her fingers. "Do you know, I believe she quite deserves my brother!"

"But, Kevin, they are gone!"

"No, no. I brought them here. They are downstairs. Your housekeeper is feeding them hot chocolate and buns."

Suddenly weak with relief, Charly began to giggle and couldn't stop. Naturally he had come to the rescue, even ordering them chocolate and buns. "Like a couple of children."

"Well, and is not that what they are?"

She wiped ineffectually at her wet cheeks with her free hand and he presented her with a large clean kerchief which she accepted with gratitude. "Th-thank you. But how? Where did you come up with them?"

"At Greenwich. I found them in the Binghams' gig, pulled up by the side of the road at Tollgate Hill." He slipped an arm about her waist, and as she put up no objection, he gave her a slight hug and went on. "It seems they were at point nonplus, your sister having refused to go on. Foolish of her, for already she was hopelessly compromised."

Charly stared at him. "Good God, why would she not?"

He shrugged. "Apparently she was overcome by guilt for deserting you, and had demanded to be brought back here. They were debating their next move when I discovered them. I thought it best to turn them about and bring them back. I told them that eloping was no way to return your aunt's hospitality, cheating her out of the wedding I suspect she longs to hold. Bella tells me her aunt had set forward great plans for her marriage to Cranford."

He hesitated, glancing at her sideways. "I thought Bella could stay with her until after the wedding and then they could come here to the farm. I daresay Ben and that female dragon of yours can care for them until I am back. Then I shall set them up someplace with some land and see that they do not starve romantically in a garret. It will spoil all their fun, I know, quite destroy their fairy tale, but someone in the family must be practical."

"But . . . but what about the lady in England?"

He smiled, that warm and delightful smile that left her feeling dizzy. "Oh, I will have a few embarrassing moments with his former father-in-law elect, but that's of no moment. Tony will not be there to face the music, which should suit him immensely."

"Then you have given your consent!"

"Now, I could hardly refuse when I do not plan to return to England alone myself."

England . . . Charly tried to follow his words. He was returning to England . . . and not alone. Her heart sank, a cold, leaden lump. Had he come only to bid her farewell? For a moment, her fingers closed on his arm as if she would prevent him from leaving her.

"There is a ship sailing in three weeks," he said, watching her closely. "And I have booked passage for two."

"You . . . and Tony?"

"Oh, no." He smiled again, a teasing light in his eyes. "How could I compel Tony to return to England when I have no intention of residing there or in Ireland myself?"

"But . . . you are sailing . . ."

"*We* are sailing, my love. A very different thing. And we have just time to make that ship. Pack your gear, horse lady."

She drew back, staring at him wildly. That glow in his eyes—the warm pressure of his arm about her waist—he meant it! Oh, she wanted to go, to be with him forever . . . but to leave her farm! Her horses, all she had worked for! What would become of Ben, of Zephyr?

"No! No, I cannot leave America!"

"You must, love."

She threw up her head, tragic but determined. "I cannot!"

His smile disappeared. "Are you telling me you do not love me?" he asked quietly, releasing her waist.

"Oh, oh no! I mean, yes, I do, but I cannot just go with you!"

"Oh." He grinned. "I see. Why, we shall be married first, of course."

"That is not it! I mean, well, of course, we would have to, but I won't leave my farm."

"You will, my girl."

"I won't."

Kevin looked at her and rubbed his chin thoughtfully. The masterful male act was not going to work. This was no weak female to bend to his will. Plainly, other methods were needed to force this Kate to surrender to him. No, not a Kate! Force would never cause Charlotte Deane to bow down to any man. And how much better than a broken-spirited Kate! Now he knew for sure this was the one woman for him. He wanted no weak, submissive female. He wanted a stubborn, proud, equal—Charly! He sighed. So much for the dominant male. Without a qualm, he abandoned Petrucchio as a misguided idiot.

"If . . . if you want me," Charly said, facing him bravely, "you will have to stay here. I will not leave."

"Nor am I asking you to." He gathered her stiff figure into his arms. "To tell the truth, I find I prefer a society where a man may earn his place through worth rather than on the chance of a lucky birth." He spoke with a whimsical smile. "But surely you cannot expect my Excalibur to make the long journey to America on his own? Will you not come with me to bring him here? I want to show you my Ireland and the horses I've told you of, so that you will know the breed for which we will aim. Only wait until your Zephyr meets my Excalibur! With his strength and her speed, we'll produce racehorses beyond your fondest dreams."

She gasped, staring at him. He grinned at her incredulous expression. "Do you not think our horses will be as happy in their marriage as we with ours? By the way, I shall see Van Bleek first thing in the morning and settle this mortgage for you."

"But . . . that is my debt, nor yours!"

"Yes, yes." Soothingly, he kissed her forehead. "I offer you no charity. It is to be a betrothal gift. I know better than to offer you diamonds and pearls. They can wait until after our wedding."

"My farm . . . you would give me my farm!" Suddenly she was terrified by the happiness that welled within her.

He raised a quizzical eyebrow. "Will it not be *our* farm? We shall need a home in America, but I hope you will also spend part of each year with me in Ireland helping to breed the hunters we will raise there."

Charly looked up at him, wonder in her eyes, her heart pounding, not daring to believe what she heard. Dreams did come true! Here was not another male to order her about, to tell her to abandon her farm, her horses! Here indeed she had found the answer to her prayers.

He chuckled softly and tipped up her chin. "Speak, love, tell me you'll have me."

There was no need for a spoken answer. Her reply showed clearly in her face. He pulled her closer, and this time she went willingly.

"I say." He released her slightly, seemingly a bit concerned. "Do you think your aunt will object if I attend my own wedding in buckskins? Finch has been unable to remove all the salmon mayonnaise from my dress breeches. No, no." He covered her lips with a hand as she opened her mouth for an indignant exclamation. "I realize she would. I do not believe Treadwell will lend me his evening togs for the affair, but I shall try Cranford. He, I am sure, will have some to spare."

The smile slowly faded in his eyes, replaced by a glow that lit a fire in Charly's heart. His lips found hers, and she doubted that anything or anyone could possibly be as happy as she. Safe at last, she laid aside her burdens and let this capable man—her Compleat Horseman—take over. Sliding her arms about his neck, she sighed with pure ecstasy. She was home, her home, secure in the warmth of the strongest yet gentlest arms she had ever known.